PLAIN
TALK
ON
Leviticus
and Numbers

PLAIN
TALK
ON
Leviticus
and Numbers

MANFORD GEORGE GUTZKE
PH. D.

ZONDERVAN
PUBLISHING HOUSE
OF THE ZONDERVAN CORPORATION
GRAND RAPIDS, MICHIGAN 49506

PLAIN TALK ON LEVITICUS AND NUMBERS
Copyright © 1981 by The Zondervan Corporation

Library of Congress Cataloging in Publication Data

Gutzke, Manford George.
    Plain talk on Leviticus and Numbers.

       1. Bible. O.T. Leviticus—Commentaries. 2. Bible. O.T. Numbers—
Commentaries. I. Title.
BS1255.3.G87   222'.1307   80-25876
ISBN 0-310-41951-4

Printed in the United States of America

CONTENTS

✝
LEVITICUS
✝

LEVITICUS 1-3
Burnt Offering

† † †

Did you know that the gospel principle of Christ carrying the burden for the believer is set forth as early in the Bible as the Old Testament book of Leviticus?

The first five books in our Bible are commonly called the Pentateuch, a Latin word meaning "five books." The second book, Exodus, is the record of events that occurred when the Hebrews came out of Egypt and started on their journey to the promised land. When they reached Mount Sinai they made camp for a considerable time while Moses went to the top of the mount to commune with God. There he received the Ten Words as the Law of God, telling what God required of man. The third book of the Pentateuch, Leviticus, explains these requirements and tells us that any violation of them is sin. God is righteous, judging and condemning sin; but He also demonstrated His graciousness in showing Moses how a sinner can come to God.

God's special way of dealing in grace with a guilty sinner is similar to the way a court deals with a violator of a traffic law. Just as someone else can pay the fine and free the offender, someone else can die for us and pay the penalty for our sin. In the ritual of worship that Moses established in the tabernacle, he showed that the sinner should bring a sacrifice for his sins. He was to bring an innocent living creature, who would be offered up to die in his place.

The gospel now tells the whole world that Christ Jesus Himself is the living sacrifice who died for us. This truth was revealed to Moses in the tabernacle. The articles of furniture and the procedure in worship pictured the eternal truth of the

9

gospel that is set forth in the latter part of the book of Exodus. The procedures to be followed by the worshiper are shown in the Book of Leviticus. Because it is impossible to represent the whole truth of Christ's sacrifice in any one illustration, several illustrations—actions representing the several aspects of the sacrifice of Christ Jesus—were offered in the procedure outlined in Leviticus.

The perfect sacrifice of Christ is shown in the offerings. There were a burnt offering, a meat offering, a peace offering, a sin offering, and a trespass offering. Each shows some aspect of what was involved when Christ Jesus died for the sinner. The burnt offering is spoken of in the first chapter of Leviticus, and it illustrates the perfect commitment of Christ in suffering. When Christ Jesus offered Himself to be our sacrifice it involved His whole life—everything about Him. One characteristic of the burnt offering was that the lamb offered was to be totally, completely consumed by fire. This represents the obedience of the Son in giving Himself without reservation for us.

The burnt offering was to be a male without blemish, just as Jesus of Nazareth was perfect. The worshiper was to offer this sacrifice of his own will; nobody was to compel him to do it. In the same way, Jesus of Nazareth came to die of His own free will. He told His disciples, "I lay down my life. I take it up again."

It was written about the worshiper:

> And he shall put his hand upon the head of the burnt offering; and it shall be accepted for him to make atonement for him (Leviticus 1:4).

When I, a sinner, come into the presence of God, I come in the grace of Jesus. When I stand before God, I voluntarily commit myself to be received of God because Christ's death on Calvary's cross was acceptable to Him.

In Leviticus 1:5 it is written that the worshiper ". . . shall kill the bullock before the Lord." Just so Christ Jesus was killed for me. Then it is further written:

> But his inwards and his legs shall he wash in water: and the priest shall burn all on the altar, to be a burnt sacrifice, an offering made by fire, of a sweet savor unto the Lord (Leviticus 1:9).

Christ Jesus held back nothing when He offered Himself: He went the whole way, even suffering death. So the Hebrews were to learn from this example that God would accept a perfect sacrifice offered willingly on their behalf.

Because the sacrifice of Jesus Christ was well pleasing to God, the worshiper would be acceptable. Since I am set free, my heart can begin to praise Him now and throughout all eternity.

LEVITICUS 4
The Sin of Ignorance

† † †

Do you realize that even though a person sins through ignorance he must deal with that sin?

Leviticus 4 gives a careful description of an offering made as atonement for the sin of ignorance, because a person might do something wrong and be unaware of it. But even when done inadvertently, sin is still sin. I may not know what I have done wrong, but God knows it. This entire chapter deals with sinning in ignorance on the part of the priest, the whole congregation, the ruler, or any one of the common people.

> Speak unto the children of Israel, saying, If a soul shall sin through ignorance against any of the commandments of the Lord concerning things which ought not to be done, and shall do against any of them: If the priest that is anointed do sin according to the sin of the people; then let him bring for his sin, which he hath sinned, a young bullock without blemish unto the Lord for a sin offering (Leviticus 4:2–3).

Here is the guidance of what the priest was to do when he committed a sin in ignorance. He was to bring in a bullock and kill it before the Lord. He was to sprinkle and pour the blood and burn the fat; the remainder was then to be burned "without the camp."

All of this is figurative, showing an aspect of the death of Christ, who Himself was put to death for sin and whose blood was poured out that God should see it. When they burned the fat they included everything: any part of His life that was helpful or honorable or good was consumed. The remainder was burned outside the camp, just as Christ Jesus Himself was despised, taken out, and put away (Hebrews 13:11–12).

And if the whole congregation of Israel sin through ignorance, and the thing be hid from the eyes of the assembly, and they have done somewhat against any of the commandments of the Lord concerning things which should not be done, and are guilty; When the sin, which they have sinned against it, is known, then the congregation shall offer a young bullock for the sin, and bring him before the tabernacle of the congregation. And the elders of the congregation shall lay their hands upon the head of the bullock before the Lord: and the bullock shall be killed before the Lord (Leviticus 4:13-15).

Just because everybody is doing something does not mean it is all right. If what everybody was doing was wrong in the sight of God, the elders were to treat that sin as though it were the sin of an individual, and God accepted their sacrifice.

Moses then discussed what should be done "when the ruler hath sinned." By a "ruler" we may think of a pastor. He can do wrong, as can a father or mother.

When a ruler hath sinned, and done somewhat through ignorance against any of the commandments of the Lord his God concerning things which should not be done, and is guilty; Or if his sin, wherein he hath sinned, come to his knowledge; he shall bring his offering, a kid of the goats, a male without blemish: And he shall lay his hand upon the head of the goat, and kill it in the place where they kill the burnt offering before the Lord: it is a sin offering (Leviticus 4:22-24).

In other words, the sin of the pastor, father, mother, teacher, or ruler is treated just like any other sin.

Many of us will feel we should be included as in verse 27:

And if any one of the common people sin through ignorance, while he doeth somewhat against any of the commandments of the Lord concerning things which ought not to be done, and be guilty; Or if his sin, which he hath sinned, come to his knowledge: then he shall bring his offering, a kid of the goats, a female without blemish, for his sin which he hath sinned. And he shall lay his hand upon the head of the sin offering, and slay the sin offering in the place of the burnt offering. And the priest shall take of the blood thereof with his finger, and put it upon the horns of the altar of burnt offering, and shall pour out all the blood thereof at the bottom of the altar. And he shall take away all the fat thereof, as the fat is taken away from off the sacrifice of peace offerings; and the priest shall burn it upon the altar for a sweet savor unto the Lord; and the priest shall make an atonement for him, and it shall be forgiven him (Leviticus 4:27-31).

Sin must be confessed before the Lord. Suppose someone
would say he did not know an action was wrong when he did
it. Now that he knows, he must bring his sin before the Lord
and offer a substitute. Thank God that that has been done for
us by One without blemish—the Lord Jesus Himself. In the
same way that the fat of a sacrifice had to be burned and
consumed, any of the things about Christ that were excep-
tional were taken outside the camp and burned in a despised
way.

What does all this figurative description mean for us? Christ
Jesus is our High Priest now in the presence of God, making
intercession: offering Himself, and atoning for our sins—even
the sins we do not know about. We bring this to our hearts
and minds and thank God. Our sin is forgiven in the grace of
God.

LEVITICUS 5–6
Trespass Offering

† † †

Do you realize that what makes something sin is not what I think of it but what God thinks of it?

In Leviticus 5 Moses discussed a new aspect in the worship of God called the trespass offering. Here the worshiper has trespassed some revealed commandment of God. But since there is more about God that we do not know than what we do know, it is possible that we could offend Him unwittingly. There are, however, some things about God that He has revealed. Here again Leviticus gives careful instructions as to what the worshipers are to do.

> And if a soul sin, and hear the voice of swearing, and is a witness, whether he hath seen or known of it; if he do not utter it, then he shall bear his iniquity (Leviticus 5:1).

In other words, if the person does wrong himself or if he is aware of someone else's wrongdoing, he becomes a party to it. If he does not report or confess this wrong, he shall bear the other's iniquity as a sin of his own. He is responsible because he saw or heard it and did nothing about it.

> Or if a soul touch any unclean thing, whether it be a carcase of an unclean beast, or a carcase of unclean cattle, or the carcase of unclean creeping things, and if it be hidden from him; he also shall be unclean, and guilty. Or if he touch the uncleanness of man, whatsoever uncleanness it be that man shall be defiled withal, and it be hid from him; when he knoweth of it, then he shall be guilty (Leviticus 5:2–3).

We do have a responsibility to be careful about these matters. It may be that at the time it happened we did not recognize it as sin, but then when we realize it we must set it right.

15

> Or if a soul swear, pronouncing with his lips to do evil, or to do good, whatsoever it be that a man shall pronounce with an oath, and it be hid from him; when he knoweth of it, then he shall be guilty in one of these (Leviticus 5:4).

In the law of Moses taking a vow was a very serious matter. If someone committed himself to do something, he was responsible to do it; if he failed to do it and someone knew that, the witness shared that responsibility with him. Moses instructed them further:

> And he shall bring his trespass offering unto the Lord for his sin which he hath sinned, a female from the flock, a lamb or a kid of the goats, for a sin offering; and the priest shall make an atonement for him concerning his sin. And if he be not able to bring a lamb, then he shall bring for his trespass, which he hath committed, two turtledoves, or two young pigeons, unto the Lord; one for a sin offering, and the other for a burnt offering (Leviticus 5:6–7).

The Lord was very gracious in making provision for the poor man. If a man was not able to bring a lamb he could bring other creatures—doves or pigeons—which were not so expensive. Moses went on to explain what should be done.

> But if he be not able to bring two turtledoves, or two young pigeons, then he that sinned shall bring for his offering the tenth part of an ephah of fine flour for a sin offering; he shall put no oil upon it, neither shall he put any frankincense thereon: for it is a sin offering. Then shall he bring it to the priest, and the priest shall take his handful of it, even a memorial thereof, and burn it on the altar, according to the offerings made by fire unto the Lord: it is a sin offering. And the priest shall make an atonement for him as touching his sin that he hath sinned in one of these, and it shall be forgiven him: and the remnant shall be the priest's, as a meat offering (Leviticus 5:11–13).

All the way through, this person's sin is his own responsibility. He was to confess it to God and bring an offering. If he was not able to bring the standard offering, he brought what he could. The important thing was that he came into the presence of God and confessed his sin. The priest was to take whatever the worshiper brought, accept it as a sin offering, burn it before the Lord, and make an atonement for him.

> If a soul commit a trespass, and sin through ignorance, in the holy things of the Lord; then he shall bring for his trespass unto

the Lord a ram without blemish . . . And he shall make amends for the harm that he hath done in the holy thing, and shall add the fifth part thereto, and give it unto the priest: and the priest shall make an atonement for him with the ram of the trespass offering, and it shall be forgiven him. And if a soul sin, and committ any of these things which are forbidden to be done by the commandments of the Lord; though he wist it not, yet is he guilty, and shall bear his iniquity. And he shall bring a ram without blemish out of the flock, with thy estimation, for a trespass offering, unto the priest: and the priest shall make an atonement for him concerning his ignorance wherein he erred and wist it not, and it shall be forgiven him. It is a trespass offering: he hath certainly trespassed against the Lord (Leviticus 5:15–19).

Leviticus 6 contains a lengthy description of what was to be done if in the course of the worshiper's conduct he had somehow cheated or lied about somebody. If he had found something that belonged to another and kept it, or in any way caused another to suffer loss, then he was to restore the principal and add a fifth thereunto as a penalty. He was to return this to the other person and bring his offering to God.

And he shall bring his trespass offering unto the Lord, a ram without blemish out of the flock, with thy estimation, for a trespass offering, unto the priest: And the priest shall make an atonement for him before the Lord: and it shall be forgiven him for any thing of all that he hath done in trespassing therein (Leviticus 6:6–7).

All this brings to mind the sober seriousness with which the whole matter of doing wrong in the sight of God was to be understood; but regardless of what the sin was, it could be forgiven. We are reminded of that wonderful promise in Scripture:

Come now, and let us reason together, saith the Lord: though your sins be as scarlet, they shall be as white as snow; though they be red like crimson, they shall be as wool (Isaiah 1:18).

LEVITICUS 6–7
Laws of Offerings

† † †

Can you understand why it is so important to be careful how we worship God?

We are living in a day when each person feels challenged to be independent in his thinking, in order that he may do anything in his own way. We say to each other, "Have it your way." People generally do not recognize how arrogant it is to think that a limited, untrained person can know what is acceptable to God. When I see parents dealing with very small children and asking them if they want to do this or that, I often think, How do they think those youngsters can possibly know what to do, since they have never been over this road before?

The only conclusion one can reach is that the public mind does not entertain the idea that God would have any desires in the matter; people have the feeling that it is up to each person to choose, and that nobody else cares. The notion that the almighty God, who created them, has any interest in them is out of their minds. They have no idea where they came from, and many have no idea where they are going; but in the meantime they feel that they may do as they please.

The crux of the whole matter is that the only thing that counts is what is pleasing to God. God was here first, and He will be here last. I live my life in God's presence, and His hand is over all things. He has revealed what He will approve and what He will not approve. The Hebrews needed this instruction to know how to worship God and how to serve Him acceptably. There was no way they, nor I, could know that in advance. To know what God wants us to do requires us

18

to know God, and He is beyond us. That is why he showed us His requirements in His Word.

From Leviticus 6:8 through the end of chapter 7, there is a description of the guidance that God gave to the people through Moses as to the procedures they should follow in making their offerings to God. It would be easy to think when I bring something to God that it does not make any difference how I do it; but it does. Some things please Him, and others displease Him. He has outlined a procedure to follow.

Leviticus 6:8–13 outlines the law of the burnt offering. The burnt offering implies the entire principle of yielding the whole being to serve God. The worshiper brought in his sacrifice—a lamb, an ox, or a bullock—and when it was offered to God it was to be totally consumed with fire. The fire was to be always burning upon the altar; it was never to go out. In other words, when the worshiper came into the presence of God he was to have in mind that his human nature was to be yielded to God to be destroyed.

The second procedure was the law of the meat or meal offering. The worshiper brought in meal, and presented it before God. We understand from our interpretation of Scripture that this was a symbol of presenting the sacrifice of Christ for our sins. His life was like fine meal that had no rough particles in it. The meal for the meat offering was baked without leaven, which is always associated with sin in the Bible. This brings to our mind that when Christ Jesus sacrificed His life to God, there was no sin in Him. When we bring our lives before God to offer them to Him, we come intending to reject all sin and repudiate anything in us that is unacceptable to Him.

In Leviticus 6:24–30 Moses set forth the law of sin offering, the sacrifice that was offered for every sin: the sin of which the worshiper was ignorant and the sin of which he was conscious. The priest offered the sacrifice, but he was to eat the flesh of this offering. Thus when we come into the presence of God, depending on the death of the Lord Jesus Christ, we are to take that truth into our own hearts. When I have in mind that Christ Jesus died for my sins, and I come into the presence of God to claim that, I too will repudiate all sin; I will want sin to be destroyed within me.

In Leviticus 7:1–10 Moses outlined the law of the trespass offering. The worshiper who had done wrong made this offering as he came into the presence of God. When I am conscious of the fact that I have sinned, I take refuge in the marvelous revelation that I have an advocate with the Father, Jesus Christ, the righteous. In Leviticus 7:11–21 Moses outlined the law of the peace offering. The flesh of that peace offering was to be offered before God with thanksgiving and it was to be eaten on the same day it was offered. But it was actually the living Christ, rather than the animal peace offering, who prompted daily communion with God.

When we put this all together, we have a complete guide for approaching God. The fire of our sincere obedience and dedication must never go out. Our manner of life is to be uniformly yielded to God in everything, with no tolerated pockets of disobedience. Trust in the efficacy of Christ's atoning death to reconcile us to God must nourish our soul continually.

In all of this, when the worshipers were to eat the sacrifice again and again, the word came that they were to eat no fat. It is understood in the Old Testament that the fat referred to excellence, human excellence. The worshipers were to partake of none of that. Their own abilities or achievements were not to be counted as the basis of their acceptance before God. They were to be accepted before God simply because the offering that had been slain was for them.

Each of these offerings indicates something about Christ Jesus. In the burnt offering He gave Himself 100 percent to His service. The shedding of blood speaks plainly about the death on Calvary. But Jesus did more than die on Calvary: His life of perfect obedience to His Father was part of His offering to God, symbolized in the meal offering without leaven. And when He offered Himself as a peace offering, which necessitated the shedding of blood, He devoted Himself again totally to the will of God. All these sacrifices had to be perfect, making Christ the only possible true sacrifice. Thus we can learn from the Book of Leviticus principles that we can follow when we come to worship God even today.

LEVITICUS 8–9

Consecration of the Priests

† † †

Do you understand how living in the will of God can begin with a definite commitment?

The matter of a believer's living in the Lord is often spoken of as being married to Him, when we consider the church as the bride and Christ as the Bridegroom. This figure helps us to realize more clearly the truth that is revealed in Leviticus 8 and 9.

Let me remind you that married life begins with the wedding—a formal, significant event. In the wedding the man and the woman commit themselves deliberately to live together as husband and wife. In Leviticus 8 and 9 the ceremony of consecration committing Israel to obey the Lord is much like a wedding ceremony.

> And the Lord spake unto Moses, saying, Take Aaron and his sons with him, and the garments, and the anointing oil, and a bullock for the sin offering, and two rams, and a basket of unleavened bread; And gather thou all the congregation together unto the door of the tabernacle of the congregation. And Moses did as the Lord commanded him; and the assembly was gathered together unto the door of the tabernacle of the congregation. And Moses said unto the congregation, This is the thing which the Lord commanded to be done (Leviticus 8:1–5).

Then followed the ceremony, first performed with Aaron and his seed in Leviticus 8, and finally with the congregation as a whole in Leviticus 9. This ceremony illustrated the truth that believers begin their lives as babies in the plan of God, dependent upon parents and other adults as they develop in childhood and youth. We learn from the guidance and exam-

21

ples of teachers, and leaders. So understanding is a matter of growth and development. In worshiping God we need help from those who know what it all means.

> For every high priest taken from among men is ordained for men in things pertaining to God, that he may offer both gifts and sacrifices for sins: Who can have compassion on the ignorant, and on them that are out of the way; for that he himself also is compassed with infirmity. And by reason hereof he ought, as for the people, so also for himself, to offer for sins. And no man taketh this honor unto himself, but he that is called of God, as was Aaron (Hebrews 5:1-4).

Since the life of a believer is grounded in faith, he should come into personal relationship with the living God so that his faith might grow. To bring this to pass, the priest, who understands God's plan, has a part to play. He guides the people in the ceremony of worshipping God. As designed by the Lord, this ceremony is performed first with the priest and then with the congregation; first with the parents, then with the children; first with the pastor, then with the church members.

> And Moses brought Aaron and his sons, and washed them with water (Leviticus 8:6).

The first thing done was to cleanse the people, to wash off all that which was unclean. In verses 7-9 Moses clothed them with garments that were specially prepared for them to make them acceptable before God. In verses 10-12 his anointing them with oil suggests that the Holy Spirit was on them, anointing them that they might respond to the presence of God.

In verse 14 Moses offered a bullock as a sin offering for the priest, who was also in need of forgiveness. Moses then sprinkled the blood on the tabernacle, making reconciliation with God on the basis of Calvary for minister, parent, and leader. In verse 16 Moses burned the fat: the repudiation of any personal worth. Verse 17 reports that the remainder was burned outside the camp, in a place normally despised.

> For the bodies of those beasts, whose blood is brought into the sanctuary by the high priest for sin, are burned without the camp. Wherefore Jesus also, that he might sanctify the people with his own blood, suffered without the gate. Let us go forth therefore unto him without the camp, bearing his reproach (Hebrews 13:11-13).

When the priests came into the presence of God they were to turn aside or burn anything that was human and personal.

In verse 18, Moses offered a ram for the burnt offering, as a sign that the priest was totally committed in his obedience to God. After Moses killed the ram, he took the blood of it and put it upon the tip of Aaron's right ear and upon the thumb of his right hand and upon the great toe of his right foot.

What does the blood signify? The blood of Christ, sacrificed for us at Calvary. The ear hears the Word of God; therefore when a person has a blood-marked ear he hears God's Word rather than the words of man. Next, Moses put blood on the thumb of the right hand, probably the greatest physical instrument for work in the world. With our hands we do many things, from working to sealing promises; their being marked with blood means that we do all as unto the Lord. Whatever we do, we do all in the name of the Lord Jesus, who loved us and gave Himself for us. Moses also put blood on the great toe of the right foot to mean that a person walks in the way of the Lord, in the way of self-sacrifice.

Thus, by ceremony the priest was dedicated to God to hear with his ears the Word of God, to work with his hands the work of God, and to walk with his feet in the way of God.

In the same way, God wants a believer in the Lord Jesus Christ to be committed to the Lord: to walk in the Lord just as if he were married to Him.

LEVITICUS 9–10
Nadab and Abihu

† † †

Do you think personal liberty, the right to do as one pleases, is permissible in serving the Lord?

Leviticus 9 gives a description of the consecration of the congregation. The word "consecration" means the setting aside for a particular purpose. The first seven verses describe the careful preparations for this stately ceremony. Then verses 8–11 describe a sin offering for Aaron. The people were to know that the priest was a sinful man who needed to be reconciled to God. In verses 12–14 the burnt offering for Aaron and his sons is described.

Verse 15 describes the various offerings for the people. The sin offering indicated reconciliation with God; the burnt offering signified the people's complete obedience to God; the meat offering implied their daily obedience; the peace offering reminded them that there was to be no contention among them; and finally, the wave offering seemed to imply offering themselves before God, asking for His guidance, as if to say: "Speak Lord, for thy servant heareth" (1 Samuel 3:9).

Finally, in verse 22, Aaron blessed the people, assuring them that God would bless them as they committed themselves to Him. Verses 23 and 24 record the Shekinah Glory, which was very impressive. When the priests and the people had been consecrated to serve God, God demonstrated His acceptance of this sacrifice by filling the tabernacle with a cloud of His glory, pointing forward to the Day of Pentecost. In the consecration of the congregation we may think again of the wedding ceremony and have the feeling that these people should have lived happily ever after.

But there is something in chapter 10 that startles us. One elemental principle is to be recognized: the worshiper does not come before God any way he pleases; he comes before God as God requires. You may wonder why that should be. Keep this in mind: a human being has no adequate conception of the person of God; he cannot know what would be acceptable to God. Because man's thinking has all the limitations of man, God has to reveal His will. It is striking to actually find out what God wants and that it is far less than man thinks it would be.

Man in his own arrogance is tempted to take liberties when he comes into the presence of God. People feel that the worship of God is to be somewhat cultural. But when they come into the presence of God they are to come the way God wants them. God will judge the people who take liberties.

This truth is set forth in Leviticus 10 in a tragedy that happened in Aaron's own family.

> And Nadab and Abihu, the sons of Aaron, took either of them his censer, and put fire therein, and put incense thereon, and offered strange fire before the Lord, which he commanded them not (Leviticus 10:1).

Nadab and Abihu came into the presence of God doing as they pleased. Their action was unacceptable, not because of some obvious, rational fact that can be pointed out, but because it was not what God asked for.

> And there went out fire from the Lord, and devoured them, and they died before the Lord (Leviticus 10:2).

No warning was given; they were just suddenly destroyed. Moses explained it to Aaron:

> This is it that the Lord spake, saying, I will be sanctified in them that come nigh me, and before all the people I will be glorified. And Aaron held his peace (Leviticus 10:3).

These men had blundered in not honoring God. He will not allow impudence, and Aaron realized it. Moses called upon two other young men to take the bodies away (10:4). Then he instructed Aaron and the others, "Uncover not your heads, neither rend your clothes; lest ye die, and lest wrath come upon all the people." There was to be no mourning for the destroyed priests, because they had offended God. But notice this at the end of verse 6, ". . .but let your brethren, the whole house of Israel, bewail the burning which the Lord hath kindled." The people could be sorry for that.

Moses told Aaron not to leave his post of duty.

> And ye shall not go out from the door of the tabernacle of the congregation, lest ye die: for the anointing oil of the Lord is upon you. And they did according to the word of Moses (Leviticus 10:7).

Aaron had a task to perform. He had been anointed by God Himself, and he was not to fail in his responsibilities. The further instruction gives a clue as to what Nadab and Abihu had done:

> And the Lord spake unto Aaron, saying, Do not drink wine nor strong drink, thou, nor thy sons with thee, when ye go into the tabernacle of the congregation, lest ye die: it shall be a statute for ever throughout your generations: And that ye may put difference between holy and unholy, and between unclean and clean (Leviticus 10:8–10).

People are to avail themselves of no stimulant when they are leading the worship of God.

The significance of the priests' conduct is that the priests teach others. This is also the case of not only the pastor, but officers and teachers in the church. And it is especially true of parents. It may be a lonely, difficult task, but it is absolutely essential that standards not be let down by those who set the examples for others.

The latter part of this chapter describes the confusion in Aaron's family and the procedure to be followed after this calamity. Moses reminded them that each had been ordained to his task, and each should proceed in his own integrity.

LEVITICUS 11–12
Clean and Unclean

† † †

Can you see the importance of exercising discrimination in this world?

One general condition in our world causes serious problems for man: good and bad things are all mixed together, making it difficult to distinguish between good and evil. Due to this difficulty, the dangerous attitude of experimentalism has become common among us today.

In moving from Egypt, where they were slaves, to Canaan, where they would be citizens, the Hebrews came into privileges and opportunities they had never had before. It was important that they should learn to exercise discrimination, to choose the good and avoid the evil. Leviticus 11 reports the way Moses prepared the people to make distinctions. He undertook to establish the principle of "clean and unclean" in daily routines as an important principle.

We who served in the military were required to polish buttons, shoes, and equipment. This practice annoyed me because I did not understand that we were being taught meticulous obedience, a lesson which could save a soldier's life. To teach these people the same meticulous obedience, Moses decreed this principle of "clean and unclean."

Leviticus 11 is plainly speaking about food, describing unclean animals in verses 2–8, and unclean fish in verses 9–12. No explanation was given for why certain fish, foul, and even insects were all right to eat and others were not. Even touching the bodies of the unclean (vv. 24–28) made a person unclean.

Moses was seeking to drive a point home: the Lord demands obedience in all areas. How important it is today for parents to train little children to be careful about things prohibited. A parent should never hesitate to say "don't"; it is a good word. If I were approaching the edge of a big cliff I would want to see not only a warning sign, but a blockade— something that says "No, not here." All of this comes to mind as we read these words:

> For I am the Lord your God: ye shall therefore sanctify yourselves, and ye shall be holy; for I am holy: neither shall ye defile yourselves with any manner of creeping thing that creepeth upon the earth. For I am the Lord that bringeth you up out of the land of Egypt, to be your God: ye shall therefore be holy, for I am holy. This is the law of the beasts, and of the fowl, and of every living creature that moveth in the waters, and of every creature that creepeth upon the earth: To make a difference between the unclean and the clean, and between the beast that may be eaten and the beast that may not be eaten (Leviticus 11:44–47).

They were to hold themselves apart and make a difference between the unclean and the clean all the way through their way of life. For us as it was for them, the route of healthy living is to be careful, avoiding the evil and choosing the good.

I remember years ago hearing a missionary tell how he tried to help a native community in a foreign country escape the ravages of a certain fever that was besetting them. He believed they were contracting this fever through drinking polluted water out of a pond which cattle drank from and waded in. The missionary explained to the people that this water was polluted, and that drinking fresh, clean water would free them from some of the ravages of the disease. When he returned later, he found that the leaders of the tribe had put a fence across one end of the pond. Thus by keeping the cattle in one section, the people could drink water out of the other section of the pond. The leaders believed that because the cattle were kept away by a fence, the polluted water would also be kept away.

But foolish as that may seem to us, consider what we tolerate in the permissiveness of our own society. We tolerate more exposure of the human body than ever before, and we allow the newstands to display obscene materials. In matters of religion, all kinds of doctrines are openly presented. We would do well to remember that the danger of infection is as real today as it was in the days of Moses. He equipped the people to realize that there were things that were unclean, improper and unacceptable to God, and he told the people how to avoid infection.

LEVITICUS 13–14

Purification and Leprosy

† † †

Have you ever wondered whether the spiritual dangers of infection are as great as the physical dangers?

Several generations ago people did not pay much attention to hygiene, and many people died in hospitals from being infected by diseases other patients had or from uncleanness in the handling of instruments. But we have made great advances in hygiene. We have a relevant proverb which says that an ounce of prevention is worth a pound of cure. In light of all this, one of the strange enigmas of our day is the public disregard of the danger of infection in matters that have to do with mental, cultural, moral, or spiritual affairs.

Our society seems to think that morals are not contagious. We send our children to schools where professors and teachers present ideas that are distinctly not according to our beliefs. The same is true with reference to spiritual matters. It is surprising how many people think that the whole matter of morals is just each individual's preference.

We know the dangers of sin. But when we fall, we are instructed that there is a way out, just as there was a way for the Israelites to become clean again.

When a woman wanted to be clean, she was to bring a lamb for a burnt offering in indication of her desire to be consecrated to God. She was to bring a pigeon or turtledove for a sin offering, indicating that she wanted to be reconciled to God. She was to turn her offerings over to the priest, who would make atonement for her, and she would be clean. In the same way Christians have an everlasting High Priest who is in the presence of God to make intercession for them.

The provision was made, if the woman had no money, that she should bring the two turtledoves or pigeons—one for the burnt offering and one for the sin offering. Because in ordinary human affairs there arose situations in which a person became unclean, he could come into the presence of the Lord with confession, claiming the sacrifice for his sins in the sin offering and presenting the sacrifice for his soul in the burnt offering. He was then reconciled to God and consecrated to walk with Him, as we are today through Christ's sacrifice.

The forgiveness of sin is one of the wonderful truths of the gospel. Some of the most gracious words ever uttered are "Neither do I condemn thee: go, and sin no more" (John 8:11). To be freely forgiven is a priceless boon. But there is great danger here that the new believer could become careless, relaxing his guard because God has freely forgiven him and set him free. It is easy to overlook the danger of being entangled again. The will of God for cleansed persons was set forth by Moses in Leviticus 13 and 14.

In setting forth the will of God concerning the cleansing of the body from leprosy, Moses gives us principles to follow in the treatment of sin—leprosy of the soul. In Leviticus 13:1–44 we have careful guidelines to be followed to detect the presence of sin. Some of its notorious traits are selfishness, jealousy, envy, pride, and apathy. Some people are gentle and courteous, so much so that they seem almost perfect. But sometimes they are proud. God resists the proud just as He gives grace to the humble. Another frequently hidden characteristic of sin is apathy about God. Some have made their profession of faith in Christ and have joined the church, but deep down they do not think about God. They take the blessing of God for granted. Sin manifests itself in different ways in different individuals.

Moses spent a long time describing the symptoms of leprosy, because a person does not stay healthy by taking for granted that he will be all right. Physical disease and sin are both infectious.

In Leviticus 13:45–46 Moses instructed that the leper, the known sinner, was to live outside the camp in isolation. This seems to teach that the sinner should not be allowed free access to company with those who want to walk spiritually with God. If we are going to walk with the Lord, we cannot walk with people who are walking away from God. We want to be courteous, kind, and gentle, but firm. The leper was to be put out of the camp, and we are to put the sinning person away from us. Even the garments worn by the leper were to be treated as unclean and burned.

What does that teach in spiritual matters? Social activities of ungodly people are to be avoided. Believers in Christ must be sensitive; they must be different. The believer should be intelligent about the fact that forgiveness is an act of God, and since God has forgiven him God is to be honored and His name is to be praised.

Leviticus 14 teaches what a person should do when he is forgiven. The first 30 verses set forth that the forgiven soul should turn to worship God. In Leviticus this was set forth in instructions about bringing offerings to the priest. But in our day this means that when we go to church we should open our hearts in listening to the minister. If he is faithful to the Word, he will capture our hearts and show us our shortcomings.

Moses instructed the people to bring two birds alive and clean. The priest was to kill one, and then dip the live bird in the blood. He sprinkled the worshiper seven times with the blood which pointed ahead to the blood of Christ who died for all believers. The people were also to wash their clothes, shave all hair off the body, and come into the camp. But the cleansed leper was to stay out of his house for seven days, being extraordinarily careful to avoid infection. After seven days he was again to shave all the hair from his body and wash his clothes and his flesh.

People today are acquainted with the germ theory of disease and recognize immediately the great importance of that kind of sterilization. But in those days, when they did not know anything about germs, they just accepted that this was how it was to be done. After seven days, the cleansed man was to bring lambs for sacrifice and meal: one lamb as a trespass offering, another for a sin offering, and another for a burnt offering. He was to put blood on his ear, finger, and foot; he was to be marked as belonging to God. He was then to take oil (which is a symbol of the Holy Spirit in Scripture) and put it on his ear, hand, and foot, and pour it on his head. And the priest should make an atonement for him, the forgiven soul, the cleansed patient. All of this was done after the person had been healed.

The fact that even the house in which the leper once lived was actually to be sanctified emphasized the importance of remaining clean. The whole matter of future conduct was to be definitely dealt with. As Jesus said to the forgiven adulteress, "Neither do I condemn thee: go, and sin no more." This business of "sinning no more" requires intelligence, thoughtfulness, and—most of all—God's guidance.

LEVITICUS 15
Danger of Contagion

† † †

Does a believer face any real danger of being affected by sin in other people?

At this point we could raise the question: Were the Israelites in any real danger of being influenced when they went into the land of Canaan? In the land of Canaan they were among pagans who had their own concept of God. The Canaanites surrounded themselves with altars which they had built and proceeded with public worship of the gods of Baal and Ashtaroth. We understand that these gods referred to natural powers and pleasures. Was there any danger of Israel being corrupted by these ideas?

That question would be equivalent to asking about a person who has accepted the Lord Jesus Christ as Savior if there is any danger that he could be influenced by the people around him? Obviously Moses believed greatly in the danger of such infection, because he took great pains to show the children of Israel how they might avoid it.

Unfortunately, when others around a person approve a certain course of action, it is easy to fall in line and do the same thing. Not only do others inspire us to act as they do, but it often follows that if they have a sickness, it will infect us. Since the discovery of causative germs we think we now know how diseases are transferred and communicated from person to person. With that we have developed a science of prevention which we call "antisepsis"—a science of preventing infection—which we ought to emulate in its spiritual application.

We need to be wise enough to realize that if isolation is a

good way to prevent disease, it can be helpful in preventing sin. This is so important today. It is a sign of the inspiration of Scripture that at a time when man did not have any under-standing of germs, Moses gave instructions to Israel that in-cluded practices in keeping with our latest scientific methods. In Leviticus 15 the first fifteen verses outline elaborate details about anyone having an issue of blood—a bleeding sore. There is no naming of this sore and no explanation of how it worked; there is just a simple declaration that if a person had that kind of trouble he was unclean and was to avoid contact with others until he healed. He was to remain in isolation seven additional days after the last evidence of illness.

Moses then outlined various specific instructions. Every bed that the infected person lay upon or every chair he sat upon was to be counted as unclean, and anyone touching it was considered unclean. Anything that touched or was touched by the person who was unclean was also unclean. Any vessel of earth, like crockery, that an unclean person touched had to be broken, and if the utensil were made of wood it had to be washed. Then when the man was healed and the issue was stopped, he was to stay in isolation seven additional days so that there would be no return of the disease. He was to wash his clothes and bathe himself before he was admitted back into the company of others. Finally, he was to bring sacrifices for an offering—a sin offering and a burnt offering —because although he had done all the practical things that were necessary, he had a relationship with God that had to be remembered and established.

All this can be true in the case of sin. As long as a person deliberately sins, he is unclean, and others should avoid him. When he stops sinning, others should wait for a trial period to see if his repentance is genuine and then rededicate him to the Lord. Also in personal, intimate situations, as we find in the latter part of this chapter, isolation for a time is often necessary. After isolation the healed person was to bring sacrifices for sin offering and burnt offering, so that he could be right before God. The priest was to make the atonement.

When we think of the priest making atonement we think of the fact that believers in Christ have a High Priest in heaven who makes atonement for them and keeps them in fellowship with God. Leviticus 15:31 is the significant verse that tells why all of this was done:

> Thus shall ye separate the children of Israel from their uncleanness; that they die not in their uncleanness, when they defile my tabernacle that is among them (Leviticus 15:31).

Believing people are to be very careful that they do not bring the evidence of sin into the presence of God, because He will not tolerate it. It is a fearful thing to fall into the hands of the living God, but the humble and contrite heart need not fear. The person who is willing to let God have His way can be very sure that God will arrange to cleanse him and keep him forever. For this assurance we praise His holy name.

LEVITICUS 16

Atonement

† † †

Can you understand how important it is for a believer to remember the basis upon which the grace of God is offered to him?

It is natural for a person to praise himself in times of success and blame himself in times of failure. Actually, he is wrong on both counts because God is the determining factor through His providence and grace. The spiritual thing for a believer to do is to refer all things to the almighty God. The blessedness of salvation does not relate to a man's virtue; it is not a matter of how good he is or how much good he has done. It is only due to the grace of God.

Because man finds it easy to forget this important truth, Moses instructed Israel concerning the Day of Atonement. The word *atone* is one word that has no roots in any other language. It is a verb that was originally a phrase: "at one." It is the verb that points to reconciliation: the bringing together of two as one. When two are together and they split for any reason, the process of bringing them together is called "atoning."

Once a year the priest was to lead the people through an elaborate procedure of worship in which they celebrated the fact that God had arranged for atonement or reconciliation.

> And the Lord said unto Moses, Speak unto Aaron thy brother, that he come not at all times into the holy place within the veil before the mercy seat, which is upon the ark; that he die not: for I will appear in the cloud upon the mercy seat (Leviticus 16:2).

Aaron was not to come just any way at just any time, because he could suffer death. Aaron's two sons, Nadab and Abihu, made that mistake. God said, "For I will appear in the cloud upon the mercy seat. Thus shall Aaron come into the holy place" (Leviticus 16:2–3). The following verses describe the elaborate procedures to be followed in coming into the presence of God. It should never be casual because it should always be related to the death of Christ on Calvary's cross. The worshiper needs to remember that the only reason he can talk directly to God is because Christ Jesus died for him. The bullock for a sin offering and ram for a burnt offering imply two things: not only did Christ die for me, but He gave Himself entirely in this sacrifice. When I am offering up that sacrifice I am to die with Christ and be yielded with Him all the way through.

> He shall put on the holy linen coat, and he shall have the linen breeches upon his flesh, and shall be girded with a linen girdle, and with the linen mitre shall he be attired: these are holy garments; therefore shall he wash his flesh in water, and so put them on (Leviticus 16:4).

Washing with water always implies the confessing and forsaking of any known sin. It is an acknowledgment that our ways of doing things are not right, and we are asking the almighty God to accept us when we repent and shed these sins. After washing himself, the worshiper is to put on the prepared garments. Just so, when coming into the presence of God. I need to be clothed with the righteousness of the Lord Jesus Christ.

Matthew records a parable of a guest being invited to a wedding feast. It was the custom in those days for the master of the house to provide wedding garments for those who would come, since many lacked proper garments of their own. It follows then that I can turn to God just as I am, and He will graciously forgive me; but when I come to worship Him I do not come covered with the grime of my daily living. I come confessing my sins, trusting in the Lord Jesus Christ and then putting on the white linen of His righteousness. Thus I can stand before God.

> And he shall take of the congregation of the children of Israel two kids of the goats for a sin offering, and one ram for a burnt offering (Leviticus 16:5).

The worshiper will go through the whole procedure and offer these kids for the sin offering.

> And Aaron shall offer his bullock of the sin offering, which is for himself, and make an atonement for himself, and for his house (Leviticus 16:6).

The priest himself was to go through this very careful detailed procedure; we too should think most carefully about coming to God. We come confessing that Christ died, that He is risen from the dead and that He lives for us. In other words, we come into the presence of God in the Lord Jesus Christ. In order to impress this upon the children of Israel, God commanded them to observe once a year this elaborate worship procedure, which was called the Day of Atonement.

> And this shall be a statute for ever unto you: that in the seventh month, on the tenth day of the month, ye shall afflict your souls, and do no work at all, whether it be one of your own country, or a stranger that sojourneth among you: For on that day shall the priest make an atonement for you, to cleanse you, that ye may be clean from all your sins before the Lord. It shall be a sabbath of rest unto you, and ye shall afflict your souls, by a statute for ever. And the priest, whom he shall anoint, and whom he shall consecrate to minister in the priest's office in his father's stead, shall make the atonement, and shall put on the linen clothes, even the holy garments: And he shall make an atonement for the holy sanctuary, and he shall make an atonement for the tabernacle of the congregation, and for the altar, and he shall make an atonement for the priests, and for all the people of the congregation. And this shall be an everlasting statute unto you, to make an atonement for the children of Israel for all their sins once a year. And he did as the Lord commanded Moses (Leviticus 16:29–34).

LEVITICUS 17–18

Lust Forbidden

† † †

Do you realize that even if a person belongs to God and so is assured of His blessing in his life, there are yet some activities that are forbidden?

The gospel offers a wonderful possibility of blessing to whosoever will believe in Him. The believer is promised forgiveness of sins, guidance in daily affairs, blessedness of fellowship with God, protection at all times, and heaven. But the believer is not changed into an angel; the flesh is never changed. If a man who has been sinking in a boggy swamp happens to come upon a rock, in stepping up on the rock he is safe. He is out of the bog, but he is no stronger than he was before; he is just better off. If he were to fall back into that bog, he would go down just as he did before. It is true that the believer is promised deliverance from sin. Sinful habits can be taken away, if he denies himself unto death. Any time he does that in faith in the Lord Jesus Christ, he will be set free.

So the believer in Christ has in himself two natures: the old man who lived according to the flesh, and the new man who lives according to the Spirit. The apostle Paul states plainly in the New Testament that as long as he lives in the flesh, the flesh is a potential threat. And that means that until he dies and passes from this world, he carries his flesh in his body.

To help the believer, God gives the Holy Spirit into the heart, and the Holy Spirit shows the things of Christ unto the believer. The Holy Spirit has the power to deliver the believer from that which is of the flesh. The Scriptures are the written Word of God as Jesus was the incarnate Word of God. The Holy Spirit teaches the Old Testament Scriptures to the believer, leading him in the will of God along the route of deliverance. So we turn to the Old Testament to learn what is written there that may teach us how to act in our day and time. Leviticus is a book of instruction to believing, delivered, and blessed people who were to live in the land of the promises of God. But they were not to be careless. And in Leviticus 17 and 18 we find that the people of God were to control their actions with responsibility:

> Speak unto Aaron, and unto his sons, and unto all the children of Israel, and say unto them; This is the thing which the Lord hath commanded, saying, What man soever there be of the house of Israel, that killeth an ox, or lamb, or goat, in the camp, or that killeth it out of the camp, And bringeth it not unto the door of the tabernacle of the congregation, to offer an offering unto the Lord before the tabernacle of the Lord; blood shall be imputed unto that man; he hath shed blood; and that man shall be cut off from among his people: to the end that the children of Israel may bring their sacrifices, which they offer in the open field, even that they may bring them unto the Lord, unto the door of the tabernacle of the congregation, unto the priest, and offer them for peace offerings unto the Lord. And the priest shall sprinkle the blood upon the altar of the Lord at the door of the tabernacle of the congregation, and burn the fat for a sweet savor unto the Lord. And they shall no more offer their sacrifices unto devils, after whom they have gone a-whoring. This shall be a statute for ever unto them throughout their generations (Leviticus 17:2–7).

We are reminded of the Scripture that says, "Thou shalt have no other gods before me" and again, "For I the Lord thy God am a jealous God" (Exodus 20:3, 5). God will not tolerate that the believer in Christ should give any sort of credit or esteem to any other being than Himself.

> And thou shalt say unto them, Whatsoever man there be of the house of Israel, or of the strangers which sojourn among you, that offereth a burnt offering or sacrifice, And bringeth it not unto the door of the tabernacle of the congregation, to offer it unto the Lord; even that man shall be cut off from among his people (Leviticus 17:8–9).

Do you realize what that is saying? The children of Israel were to count that man out and not have fellowship with him.

> And whatsoever man there be of the house of Israel, or of the strangers that sojourn among you, that eateth any manner of

blood; I will even set my face against that soul that eateth blood, and will cut him off from among his people (Leviticus 17:10).

After the doings of the land of Egypt, wherein ye dwelt, shall ye not do: and after the doings of the land of Canaan, whither I bring you, shall ye not do: neither shall ye walk in their ordinances. Ye shall do my judgments, and keep mine ordinances, to walk therein: I am the Lord your God. Ye shall therefore keep my statutes, and my judgments: which if a man do, he shall live in them: I am the Lord (Leviticus 18:3–5).

This is stern instruction, as plain as day. Once they lived in the land of Egypt, surrounded by all kinds of pagan ideas. But they were coming into a new land, and they would live on a new spiritual level in which they could have fellowship with God. But even here there would be evil forces and people who lived contrary to God, who would lead them astray. If they lived according to the popular notion of those pagan people and went contrary to the things of God, they would be cut off.

After verse 5 follow sundry descriptions of illicit behavior, which is never acceptable to God. One can appreciate the fine restraint in description as well as the direct meaning. As we read this we become aware that men have natural desires that arise within the flesh. In themselves these desires are what we would call amoral: they are neither good or bad. The fact that these desires arise in a person merely marks him as a human being. But he is responsible to restrict his actions from being motivated by such desires. Any human being living in this world can be tempted. Even the Lord Jesus was tempted. But when any person yields to temptation he sins.

Defile not ye yourselves in any of these things: for in all these the nations are defiled which I cast out before you: And the land is defiled: therefore I do visit the iniquity thereof upon it, and the land itself vomiteth out her inhabitants. Ye shall therefore keep my statutes and my judgments, and shall not commit any of these abominations; neither any of your own nation, nor any stranger that sojourneth among you: (For all these abominations have the men of the land done, which were before you, and the land is defiled;) That the land spew not you out also, when ye defile it, as it spewed out the nations that were before you. For whosoever shall commit any of these abominations, even the souls that commit them shall be cut off from among their people. Therefore shall ye keep mine ordinance, that ye commit not any one of these abominable customs, which were committed before you, and that ye defile not yourselves therein: I am the Lord your God (Leviticus 18:24–30).

This is a very sobering warning. In the world all round about us there are all kinds of ideas which are attractive and, on occasion, sound reasonable. But the Scriptures warn us that we are to go only the way that is revealed in the Word of God in order to be acceptable to Him.

LEVITICUS 19–20
Control Conduct

† † †

Do you think that if a person accepts Jesus Christ as his Savior and Lord, his manner of life should conform to a revealed standard from God?

It is common to feel that the fullness of life should include personal liberty. That may sound good, but it is not the truth. The believer in Christ does not have the privilege of doing as he pleases just because he belongs to the Lord. The notion of personal liberty with freedom to choose according to personal preference is not what the Bible teaches. That idea has persisted because it is so agreeable to the natural man.

However, the gospel presents the truth that a believer is free from all other men but never free from God. The Apostle Paul described himself as "being not without law to God, but under the law to Christ" (1 Corinthians 9:21). He was free so far as the law was concerned in this world, but he was always subject to God. Although believers do not obey the law as a means to be blessed, they follow the law as a guide because they want to please God.

This is brought out as we continue our study in Leviticus.

> Speak unto all the congregation of the children of Israel, and say unto them, Ye shall be holy: for I the Lord your God am holy (Leviticus 19:2).

The requirement is that the worshiper be 100 percent turned over to God, because he belongs to God. The Hebrews were to be holy in order that they might get out of Egypt, but they were also to be holy in order that they might be blessed in the land of Canaan. God promised to take them across the desert and into the land of Canaan; but when they reached the land

of Canaan, they were to walk in the ways of God that they
might be blessed.

Leviticus 19 contains a number of simple, clear directions
that are based on the Ten Words.

> And if ye offer a sacrifice of peace offerings unto the Lord, ye
> shall offer it at your own will (Leviticus 19:5).

The peace offerings were required, but a person was not to
bring the sacrifice into the presence of God as a response to an
obligation; he was to come in of his own free will. Coming of
his own free will did not mean he could do as he pleased, but
it meant that he could walk in the ways that God had outlined.

> It shall be eaten the same day ye offer it, and on the morrow:
> and if aught remain until the third day, it shall be burnt in the
> fire (Leviticus 19:6).

This procedure was to be kept up day by day. There was to be
no such thing as a person's being godly on Monday, and then
doing as he pleased all the rest of the week. He was to be
godly all the time.

> And if it be eaten at all on the third day, it is abominable; it
> shall not be accepted. Therefore every one that eateth it shall
> bear his iniquity, because he hath profaned the hallowed thing
> of the Lord: and that soul shall be cut off from among his people
> (Leviticus 19:7–8).

God dealt with His people consistently in all areas. These
matters did not rise out of each other; they are strung together
like beads on a string. They have one principle woven all the
way through: the believer, the child of God, does not do as he
pleases. He is guided of God. The marvelous thing is that
when his heart is right with God he wants to please Him. He
needs only to know what the will of God is; then he will do it.

> And when ye reap the harvest of your land, thou shalt not
> wholly reap the corners of thy field, neither shalt thou gather
> the gleanings of thy harvest. And thou shalt not glean thy
> vineyard, neither shalt thou gather every grape of thy vine-
> yard; thou shalt leave them for the poor and stranger: I am the
> Lord your God (Leviticus 19:9–10).

The worshiper was not to take everything for himself. He was
to remember the poor and the stranger.

Thou shalt not curse the deaf, nor put a stumbling block before the blind, but shalt fear thy God: I am the Lord. Ye shall do no unrighteousness in judgment: thou shalt not respect the person of the poor, nor honor the person of the mighty: but in righteousness shalt thou judge thy neighbor. Thou shalt not go up and down as a talebearer among thy people: neither shalt thou stand against the blood of thy neighbor: I am the Lord. Thou shalt not hate thy brother in thine heart: thou shalt in any wise rebuke thy neighbor, and not suffer sin upon him. Thou shalt not avenge, nor bear any grudge against the children of thy people, but thou shalt love thy neighbor as thyself: I am the Lord (Leviticus 19:14–18).

They were to exercise this kind of control in their daily life.

And if a stranger sojourn with thee in your land, ye shall not vex him. But the stranger that dwelleth with you shall be unto you as one born among you, and thou shalt love him as thyself; for ye were strangers in the land of Egypt: I am the Lord your God (Leviticus 19:33–34).

We should be careful about that in our churches. The Lord wants us to treat that newcomer as one who was born there. "For ye were strangers in the land of Egypt."

Ye shall do no unrighteousness in judgment, in meteyard, in weight, or in measure. Just balances, just weights, a just ephah, and a just hin, shall ye have: I am the Lord your God, which brought you out of the land of Egypt (Leviticus 19:35–36).

When you deal with people, be fair, honest, and reliable because "I am the Lord your God" says the Lord.

Moses continued all through Leviticus 20 in the same vein. Notice when you read verses 7 and 8, "Sanctify yourselves therefore, and be ye holy: for I am the Lord your God." This matter of being holy is a matter that calls for 100 percent commitment. "And ye shall keep my statutes, and do them: I am the Lord which sanctify you." The children of Israel were definitely committed to act differently from pagan people. They were to live in a country that was worldly; they could not possibly claim that it was godly. But they were not to act the way the pagans did. They were to be humble where the pagans were proud; honest where they were deceitful; faithful where they were false; kind where they were harsh; helpful where they were selfish. They were to maintain different attitudes from other people for God's sake.

LEVITICUS 21–22

Laws to Govern Priests

† † †

Do you think that a priest should be under stricter rules for living than the average believer?

People need to be led, and that means there must be leaders. Leading others calls for special ability and special responsibilities. Israel was led in their national life by prophets, priests, and kings. A prophet was a person who presented the Word of God to the people; a priest was one who presented the people to God; and a king was one who directed the people and the affairs of the nation under God.

It is easy for us to see the pastor as a priest, but we must also see parents, teachers, elders, friends, and witnesses as priests, because Revelation teaches that He has made us all kings and priests unto God. Inasmuch as I seek to win others, to pray for others, or to comfort others I serve as a priest. And the instructions outlined by Moses for the priests are directly suited to me as a believer.

In the first four verses of Leviticus 21 we see that the priest was not to do menial tasks for people generally, except for his own kin and in charity toward those who were destitute.

> And the Lord said unto Moses, Speak unto the priests the sons of Aaron, and say unto them, There shall none be defiled for the dead among his people: but for his kin, that is near unto him, that is, for his mother, and for his father, and for his son, and for his daughter, and for his brother, and for his sister a virgin, that is nigh unto him, which hath had no husband; for her may he be defiled. But he shall not defile himself, being a chief man among his people, to profane himself (Leviticus 21:1–4).

More specific things were then pointed out:

47

> They shall not make baldness upon their head, neither shall
> they shave off the corner of their beard, nor make any cuttings
> in their flesh (Leviticus 21:5).

These were all signs of pagan activities, which no believing
person was to imitate.

> They shall be holy unto their God, and not profane the name of
> their God: for the offerings of the Lord made by fire, and the
> bread of their God, they do offer: therefore they shall be holy
> (Leviticus 21:6).

Moses then outlined even more specific instructions, all of
which indicate that the person who is serving as a teacher or
leader should be very careful of his conduct. We read that the
priest was not to imitate pagan practices, and the worshiper
was not to act like a pagan.

Moses also dealt with matters that were very personal.

> They shall not take a wife that is a whore, or profane; neither
> shall they take a woman put away from her husband: for he is
> holy unto his God. Thou shalt sanctify him therefore; for he
> offereth the bread of thy God: he shall be holy unto thee: for I
> the Lord, which sanctify you, am holy (Leviticus 21:7–8).

So a priest in his personal life was to be very careful not to
marry an immoral woman.

> And the daughter of any priest, if she profane herself by playing
> the whore, she profaneth her father: she shall be burnt with fire
> (Leviticus 21:9).

If a daughter disgraced her father who was a priest, she was to
be destroyed. The man who was anointed to serve as a priest
was permitted to be involved in no other activities.

His married life also was to be under supervision.

> And he shall take a wife in her virginity. A widow, or a divorced
> woman, or profane, or a harlot, these shall he not take: but he
> shall take a virgin of his own people to wife (Leviticus
> 21:13–14).

The Lord gave specific qualifications a priest must have to
serve him.

> Speak unto Aaron, saying, Whosoever he be of thy seed in their
> generations that hath any blemish, let him not approach to
> offer the bread of his God. For whatsoever man he be that hath
> a blemish, he shall not approach: a blind man, or a lame, or he

> that hath a flat nose, or any thing superfluous, or a man that is broken-footed, or broken-handed, or crookbacked, or a dwarf, or that hath a blemish in his eye, or be scurvy, or scabbed, or hath his stones broken; no man that hath a blemish of the seed of Aaron the priest shall come nigh to offer the offerings of the Lord made by fire: he hath a blemish; he shall not come nigh to offer the bread of his God (Leviticus 21:17–21).

Many might feel that this is too severe, but it was intended to teach something. The man who would take the offerings of the Lord, bring and offer them, was actually acting in the place of our great High Priest, the Messiah, the Lord Jesus Christ, who lived a perfect life. When He came into the presence of God He was One in whom the Father delighted because He had always done right. Any person serving as a priest had to have no visible defects in order to convey the principle that something less than perfect would be unacceptable. We are to keep in mind that so far as the gospel of the Lord Jesus Christ and the saving power of God are concerned, it is God's great glory that His grace should extend to everybody—whosoever will may come. God is no respecter of persons—Christ Jesus died for all.

As we see these restrictions placed on those who were to serve as priests and public leaders in the Old Testament, we should keep in mind that the New Testament teaches that anyone who comes to God will not be cast out. All who are committed to the Lord partake of the righteousness of the Lord Jesus Christ. The Apostle Paul had a thorn in the flesh, but that did not hinder him from serving the Lord. As a matter of fact, he gloried in his infirmities because when he was weak, the Lord was glorified more.

Leviticus 22 is similar but with more specific instructions about how the priest was to conduct himself. He was to be as careful in conducting himself as Moses was to be careful in choosing him. We read:

> Speak unto Aaron and to his sons, that they separate themselves from the holy things of the children of Israel, and that they profane not my holy name in those things which they hallow unto me: I am the Lord. Say unto them, Whosoever he be of all your seed among your generations, that goeth unto the holy things, which the children of Israel hallow unto the Lord, having his uncleanness upon him, that soul shall be cut off from my presence: I am the Lord (Leviticus 22:2–3).

In addition to avoiding contact with the unclean, in verse 8 Moses instructed that the priest should be careful that the food he eats is clean. The priest's family might eat of his food, but if any priest eat food that is not for him, he was to pay a fine. Great care was to be exercised about offerings. The thanksgiving offering was to be carefully selected, and it was to be voluntary.

> Therefore shall ye keep my commandments, and do them: I am the Lord. Neither shall ye profane my holy name; but I will be hallowed among the children of Israel: I am the Lord which hallow you. That brought you out of the land of Egypt, to be your God: I am the Lord (Leviticus 22:31-33).

LEVITICUS 23

Feasts

† † †

Can you see the importance of having special days and special seasons to emphasize historical facts?

Because people are prone to forget, it is common for us to cherish photos and souvenirs and to commemorate special events by creating holidays. In the same way, Moses instructed the Hebrews to have certain annual feasts and fasts.

> Six days shall work be done: but the seventh day is the sabbath of rest, a holy convocation; ye shall do no work therein: it is the sabbath of the Lord in all your dwellings (Leviticus 23:3).

God's plan was that the curse that was put upon Adam in the Garden of Eden was upon all mankind, so that man has to work in this world. God's plan is that the curse should eventually be lifted. So every seven days we are given a glimpse of that; we are reminded of God's plan. Every seven days there is to be a day without work.

Leviticus 23:4–8 describes the Passover Feast, which celebrates the fact that the believer is reconciled to God. I now have the privilege of turning to God not because I am good, but because Christ Jesus died for me. Our counterpart of the Passover Feast is the sacrament of the Lord's Supper, which we are to do in remembrance of the Lord Jesus.

In Leviticus 23:9–14 we have an interesting celebration of the first fruits at the beginning of the harvest. Before any of the harvest was eaten, they were to set some of it aside unto the Lord. They were to praise the Lord for His goodness.

In Leviticus 23:15–21 Moses described the harvest home which was celebrated fifty days after the first fruits. Our spir-

itual counterpart is the Day of Pentecost. This Feast of First
Fruits pointed forward to the resurrection of Jesus, which was
followed (fifty days later) by Pentecost in the coming of the
Holy Spirit. This is the harvest Jesus reaped when He was put
into the ground as seed is planted, when He was put to death
and died for us on the cross.

When we have committed ourselves to God and He has
blessed us and surrounded us with His favor, we should share
this with others. We should not be selfish with the blessings of
God; we should share with others.

> And when ye reap the harvest of your land, thou shalt not make
> clean riddance of the corners of thy field when thou reapest,
> neither shalt thou gather any gleaning of thy harvest: thou shalt
> leave them unto the poor, and to the stranger: I am the Lord
> your God (Leviticus 23:22).

Leviticus 23:23–25 emphasizes the Feast of Trumpets—a service of thanksgiving and praise. "Ye shall do no servile work
therein: but ye shall offer an offering made by fire unto the
Lord" to signify total obedience. When worshipers come into
the presence of God to thank and praise Him, it would be a
hollow exercise if they did not have the idea "Here am I Lord,
send me."

Leviticus 23:26–32 describes the atonement as very sober
and serious. The worshipers were to take time out to think of
the cost of the sacrifice that had been offered on their behalf.

> . . .And ye shall afflict your souls, and offer an offering made by
> fire unto the Lord. And ye shall do no work in that same day:
> for it is a day of atonement, to make an atonement for you
> before the Lord your God. For whatsoever soul it be that shall
> not be afflicted in that same day, he shall be cut off from among
> his people. And whatsoever soul it be that doeth any work in
> that same day, the same soul will I destroy from among his
> people (Leviticus 23:27–30).

The Feast of Tabernacles was then described in Leviticus
23:33–43. For seven days the whole congregation was to go
out from their homes and dwell in booths.

> These are the feasts of the Lord, which ye shall proclaim to be
> holy convocations, to offer an offering made by fire unto the
> Lord, a burnt offering, and a meat offering, a sacrifice, and
> drink offerings, every thing upon his day: beside the sabbaths

of the Lord, and beside your gifts, and beside all your vows, and beside all your freewill offerings, which ye give unto the Lord . . . And ye shall rejoice before the Lord your God seven days . . . Ye shall dwell in booths . . . That your generations may know that I made the children of Israel to dwell in booths, when I brought them out of the land of Egypt: I am the Lord your God (Leviticus 23:37–43).

The booths were apparently like tents, temporary structures. The people were to go out from their homes and live in open territory that they might be reminded how it was when they crossed the desert.

Thus we see how the people who were believers were to take measures to remember the great things God had done. May you and I be given grace to do that very thing: to remember that the Lord Jesus Christ came to die for us that we might be saved.

LEVITICUS 24
Conformity Desired

†　†　†

Can you understand why there should be the same penalty for any infraction of the law?

In assessing penalties for any crime we tend to look at the wrongdoer, and then gauge the penalty to suit him; but this is really getting off on the wrong foot. We must not forget that when our society was established the Bible was the inspiration and the norm of our laws. Our founders were governed by what the Bible said. Later men began to think that the first laws were only the judgment of the first men, and so they felt free to change laws to suit themselves. Today one need only listen to the radio or television, or read the newspapers to learn that the general opinions expressed are those of men in whose thinking there is no God.

When crime is evaluated in the human situation, it is in terms of human beings with an entirely different point of view from that found in the Scriptures. Moses reminded the people that the Lord was present, and all crime was against Him personally. Judgment was not to be based on who committed the crime but on the crime itself, because it was committed against God.

> And the Lord spake unto Moses, saying, Command the children of Israel, that they bring unto thee pure oil olive beaten for the light, to cause the lamps to burn continually. Without the veil of the testimony, in the tabernacle of the congregation, shall Aaron order it from the evening unto the morning before the Lord continually: it shall be a statute for ever in your generations. He shall order the lamps upon the pure candlestick before the Lord continually (Leviticus 24:1–4).

Do you notice how the word *continually* occurs again and

again? The lamps were to burn as a constant testimony to the Lord. Also cakes with frankincense were to be set out repeatedly in an orderly fashion as a burnt offering.

> Every sabbath he shall set it in order before the Lord continually, being taken from the children of Israel by an everlasting covenant. And it shall be Aaron's and his sons'; and they shall eat it in the holy place: for it is most holy unto him of the offerings of the Lord made by fire by a perpetual statute (Leviticus 24:8-9).

The Lord is entitled to the service and the praise of His people all the time. In the tabernacle they burned candles which symbolized praise to God. As those flames rose, so their hands were to go up with praise toward God, again and again.

Leviticus 24:10-16 records an incident in which the half-breed son of an Israelite woman cursed God in strife. He went among the children of Israel and "blasphemed the name of the Lord and cursed." He was arrested and put in prison to await the penalty. Such an incident had never occurred before, and a new regulation was spelled out to reveal the mind of the Lord.

> And he that blasphemeth the name of the Lord, he shall surely be put to death, and all the congregation shall certainly stone him: as well the stranger, as he that is born in the land, when he blasphemeth the name of the Lord, shall be put to death (Leviticus 24:16).

The congregation was to carry out this sentence. It was not a matter of paying back the criminal; he blasphemed God and he paid the penalty.

> And he that killeth any man shall surely be put to death. And he that killeth a beast shall make it good; beast for beast (Leviticus 24:17-18).

In these cases, however, there was to be restitution. If one man killed another man's ox, he was to pay for it.

> Ye shall have one manner of law, as well for the stranger, as for one of your own country: for I am the Lord your God. And Moses spake to the children of Israel, that they should bring forth him that had cursed out of the camp, and stone him with stones. And the children of Israel did as the Lord commanded Moses (Leviticus 24:22-23).

Wrong was judged in the sight of God and there was a penalty, regardless of who did it. The sentence of death by stoning was carried out by the congregation as a judgment for sin. All believers should join in judging sin, never excusing or tolerating it.

LEVITICUS 25-26
Living in the Land

† † †

Does it make sense that even though God's grace is free and rich, the response of the believer should be careful and controlled?

One line of thought prevails in Leviticus 25 and 26: man must not carelessly presume upon the kindness of God. The children of Israel living in the land of Canaan were extraordinarily blessed above all other mankind. They came into possession of farms which they had neither worked nor paid for. They had promises from God that blessing would be theirs. They had good crops and they enjoyed peace. But because of their great blessing, they were confronted with a great challenge and responsibility. Being in God's presence required of them that they do everything according to His will, for which Moses gave them careful instructions.

The first seven verses of Leviticus 25 have to do with the land they would be cultivating. The law was that the land was to have a sabbath of rest:

> Six years thou shalt sow thy field, and six years thou shalt prune thy vineyard, and gather in the fruit thereof; but in the seventh year shall be a sabbath of rest unto the land, a sabbath for the Lord: thou shalt neither sow thy field, nor prune thy vineyard. That which groweth of its own accord of thy harvest thou shalt not reap, neither gather the grapes of thy vine undressed: for it is a year of rest unto the land (Leviticus 25:3-5).

My father was a farmer in Canada and was successful in handling his farm by following a practice called summer fallowing. In this procedure a field of his would be allowed to lie fallow for one year. Only plowing would be done to kill weeds. This proved to be wise farming. Thus, I was very interested to learn that Moses had prescribed this very procedure for Israel many generations ago.

The people were to observe a jubilee year every fifty years. The sabbath year came every seven years, so that in forty-nine years they would have had seven sabbaths; but the fiftieth year was a jubilee year. This was most interesting. Even when the land had been sold or a man had sold himself as a slave to pay off a debt, in the jubilee year all slaves went free, all land was returned to the original owner, and all debts were cancelled.

When I heard in my own lifetime about a moratorium in debts (about the possibility that our economy would be helped if every now and then there would be a cancellation of all debts), I had no idea that this was actually embedded in the Old Testament. By this remarkable procedure the people were blessed. This might not have seemed fair to some, but it was very practical. The result of that principle was that the rich did not become too rich, and the poor did not become too poor. This was done by God's people under God's guidance.

> And if ye shall say, What shall we eat the seventh year? behold, we shall not sow, nor gather in our increase: then I will command my blessing upon you in the sixth year, and it shall bring forth fruit for three years (Leviticus 25:20–21).

If the land was sold at any time, the right of redemption would always be included. The seller could always buy it back if the time came that he had the money. If a brother got into debt so that he became a bondsman (a slave), he would always have the privilege of buying back his freedom, or being redeemed. Moses included instructions as to how he was to be treated.

> And as a yearly hired servant shall he be with him: and the other shall not rule with rigor over him in thy sight (Leviticus 25:53).

This meant that if a certain Israelite sold himself to work to pay off a debt, the brother who controlled him was not to treat him cruelly.

> Ye shall make you no idols nor graven image, neither rear you up a standing image, neither shall ye set up any image of stone in your land, to bow down unto it: for I am the Lord your God. Ye shall keep my sabbaths, and reverence my sanctuary: I am the Lord (Leviticus 26:1–2).

Moses then set out the marvelous truth that obedience will bring blessing.

> If ye walk in my statutes, and keep my commandments, and do them . . . I will walk among you, and will be your God, and ye shall be my people (Leviticus 26:3–12).

But disobedience will bring the severe chastisement of God.

> But if ye will not hearken unto me, and will not do all these commandments . . . I also will do this unto you; I will even appoint over you terror, consumption, and the burning ague, that shall consume the eyes, and cause sorrow of heart: and ye shall sow your seed in vain, for your enemies shall eat it. And I will set my face against you . . . And if ye will not yet for all this hearken unto me, then I will punish you seven times more for your sins . . . And if ye walk contrary unto me, and will not hearken unto me; I will bring seven times more plagues upon you according to your sins. I will also send wild beasts among you, which shall rob you of your children, and destroy your cattle, and make you few in number; and your high ways shall be desolate. And if ye will not be reformed by me by these things, but will walk contrary unto me; then will I also walk contrary unto you, and will punish you yet seven times for your sins . . . And if ye will not for all this hearken unto me, but walk contrary unto me; then I will walk contrary unto you also in fury (Leviticus 26:14–28).

But then in speaking of the children of those who have been punished, Moses tells of the grace of God.

> If they shall confess their iniquity, and the iniquity of their fathers, with their trespass which they trespassed against me, and that also they have walked contrary unto me . . . if then their uncircumcised hearts be humbled, and they then accept of the punishment of their iniquity: then will I remember my covenant with Jacob, and also my covenant with Isaac, and also my covenant with Abraham will I remember; and I will re-member the land. The land also shall be left of them, and shall enjoy her sabbaths . . . And yet for all that . . . I will not cast them away, neither will I abhor them, to destroy them utterly, and to break my covenant with them: for I am the Lord their God. But I will for their sakes remember the covenant of their ancestors . . . I am the Lord (Leviticus 26:40–45).

This sobering chapter ends thus:

> These are the statutes and judgments and laws, which the Lord made between him and the children of Israel in mount Sinai by the hand of Moses (Leviticus 26:46).

This excellent outline points out that nobody, even God's own people, should ever carelessly presume upon the kindness of God; but people must walk in repentance before Him, trusting in the mercy and the grace of God.

LEVITICUS 27

Vows to Be Kept

† † †

Do you realize that if a believer pledges anything, he cannot change his mind with God's approval after the operation is under way?

At this point in our study one thought comes to mind: while a person may have in mind that he is going to follow God and do what He wants him to do, it isn't that simple. Situations arise in which a person faces problems that he has never faced before. He needs to seek guidance from God in prayer and in meditation, that he may be led to take godly action.

Many of our activities are routine and do not require a major decision each time. These activities may be unwise, and often may cause us to sin.

In order to guide the people of Israel and to keep them from falling into wrong habits, the Lord led Moses to reveal certain patterns of conduct from time to time. We shall notice in Leviticus 27 a certain line of thought that Moses followed to guide the people, when someone proved irresponsible in fulfilling a pledge.

Irresponsibility is a common human trait that is not acceptable to God. The Word of God warns a person not to pledge himself too quickly; but when the pledge is made and the responsibility assumed, the performance is to be carried through as outlined.

Leviticus 27 draws attention to pledges or agreements between people. The first eight verses deal with a man pledging his services to work out a debt. Moses detailed the going rate by maintaining that any man between twenty and sixty years of age has a certain monetary value attached to his service. If he were from five to twenty years of age it would be somewhat less, and if he were older it was also less. If a person wanted to be free, but did not have quite enough money to buy out, the priest was to arbitrate and assess an amount that he could pay. All of this was done so that relationship between people would be worked out in an orderly way.

From verses 9 to 13 there were similar rules that covered the pledging of animals. A person could contract to turn his ox over to a neighbor to work for a certain length of time. Then if the owner wanted to get the ox back for his own service, he could go to the man to whom he had pledged the ox and pay to get it back. In verses 14 and 15 this same practical rule is followed with reference to a house. Moses said it could be pledged, but it could be redeemed again. If the owner rented the house out and then wanted to occupy it himself, he could buy up the lease at a price set by the priest. To whatever price the priest set, a 20 percent bonus was added for the privilege of redeeming it. In verses 16 to 25 a field could be pledged, or it could be sanctified—set aside unto the Lord. The owner could redeem his property by paying whatever it was worth and adding a 20 percent bonus.

The Israelites also were told that the firstborn of any living thing—animal or man—belonged to the Lord, as did all of the tithe of the land. If the man wanted to redeem the tithe— suppose the particular fruit or grain he wanted to use himself—he could buy it. He could go to the priest, pay the price and add 20 percent. This applied to the tithes of the field, of the herd, and of the flock.

These practical regulations in the last chapter of Leviticus are in the Bible to make sure that the Israelites' conduct was controlled. We notice in all these careful regulations that there was to be integrity of commitment.

CONCLUSION
Holiness Is Necessary
for Blessing

✝   ✝   ✝

Do you realize that God will not bless any who are not in His will?

One of the great attractions in the gospel is the promise of God's blessing. Man in all his weakness, in all his sinfulness, in all his uselessness can be blessed with the rich, full, wonderful blessing of the almighty God. Every human being who is conscious and sane wants the blessing of God, which gives peace, rest, protection, and safety. If the believer has suffering, God will give him strength to endure it. God will be with him in the deep water; God will watch over him and keep him. Being blessed of God gives a person strength to endure, to persist, to believe, to serve, and to hope.

And the blessing of God controls providence for good. The eyes of the Lord run to and fro over the whole earth to show Himself strong on behalf of them that trust in Him. A person who believes in God and trusts Him will be quiet, safe, able, and fortunate. He can have every good thing, by the power of God. But God exercises that power as He wills. It is not automatic. God is a living Being who wills to bless only those who do His will. People who are disobedient, careless, and selfish will not get anywhere with God. We know that God resists the proud and that He will not despise the humble and the contrite heart.

We hear little about the fact that the requirement to be willing to do His will is usually called holiness, but it has great importance. It is easy to get the impression that holiness may be desirable but not absolutely necessary. It is also easy to get the impression that holiness is something to aim for eventually, so that someday when we are no longer of this world, and when we have been made different, then we will be holy. But the Lord says that without holiness no man shall see Him.

It is possible that we need to adjust our whole idea of holiness. Holiness is not so much a goal toward which we are to improve ourselves as it is a consequence of having yielded ourselves in response to His call. The Lord God called His people and said, "Be ye holy" (Leviticus 20:7). What does that mean? Does this mean that a person shall enter into a process of self-discipline so that he will never do wrong and then he will be holy? No, because that would never succeed. But holiness does indicate the measure of my commitment at the outset, because it results in activities and attitudes that people can properly call holiness.

Holiness itself is the fruit of total surrender to God at the beginning. "Holy" is the derivative of the English word "wholly," and it points to total response to the call of God. God expects everything to be turned over to Him; He looks to see whether there are any reservations.

Turning to God with no reservations, totally yielded, is like getting into a rowboat. It will not do for me to have one foot in the boat and one foot on the shore. That is a good way to get wet. But when I put my whole weight into the boat then I can balance it. Thus it is with the Lord. You get inside the ark, and God shuts the door on you. Moses helped Israel to do this in this Book of Leviticus by spelling out the proper total response to God in many different situations.

The word "sanctify" is often used in relation to holiness. To sanctify anything means to set it apart for a special service. When you set aside any object for a special purpose, you can properly say that object is sanctified for that purpose.

"Dedicate" is similar in its meaning and in its bearing. It goes beyond "sanctify" because it develops the next step after sanctification. When I dedicate something I commit that something to a specific use. From several pails I pick a certain one and I separate it from the rest; it is in that sense sanctified. Then I use it for a particular purpose and, in so doing, I dedicate the pail to this particular use.

Being holy is a matter of deliberate choice. The text should be: "I do always those things that please my Father."

NUMBERS

NUMBERS 1–4
Order

† † †

Do you realize that orderliness is right?

A good many of us seldom look into the Book of Numbers, but God has revealed many things there for us. It is Moses' teachings to the people of Israel, to enable them to live successfully when they were delivered from bondage in Egypt. Between Egypt, where they were slaves, and Canaan, where they were to be free citizens, was a broad expanse of desert. This was to serve as their training area. Sometime after they had escaped from Egypt and learned some basic truths in the desert, they came to Mount Sinai. Here they stayed for a while as they received instructions designed to prepare them to live freely in Canaan.

The Book of Numbers reveals instructions for instilling order in their activities. "Order" is the condition of each thing being in its place; the opposite of order is chaos. Just as in the beginning "the earth was without form, and void" (Genesis 1:2), the Scriptures tell us that that was "chaos." "And God said, Let there be light" (Genesis 1:3), creating structure out of chaos. So as Hebrews 11:3 says, "Through faith we understand that the worlds were framed by the word of God." The word "framed" suggests a structure.

To understand Numbers better, let us consider the spontaneous appearance of structure. Structure does not always occur by putting parts together little by little. It often appears spontaneously in the actual practical affairs of the world. When you have seen snowflakes you may have wondered about the amazing symmetrical structures found in each one. They appear out of the snow—out of the mist and water in the air—and each is perfect. Have you seen frost on a window? All those designs came spontaneously.

Now let us further consider crystalization. When a compound with sugar in it is cooked, it will crystalize: how does that happen? When the crystals show six or eight sides, how do they appear? Why are they always the same in symmetry? They come spontaneously. Also, consider how a flower comes out of the stem: where does the design come from? Many trees grow in the forest where they are able to grow naturally without interference, and all develop a symmetry. Where does it come from? Why are our fingers and toes where they are? The elements that form these members all come from the same food. Then how does this take place? This is God's work: He creates order so that it often appears spontaneously.

Something like this is recorded in Numbers.

> Take ye the sum of all the congregation of the children of Israel . . . from twenty years old and upward, all that are able to go forth to war in Israel (Numbers 1:2–3).

Moses was instructed to take a census of all the people and to give certain tasks to certain persons.

Numbers 2 gives the ground plan of the camp where they were to live. The tabernacle was in the center with three tribes to the east, three to the south, three to the west, and three to the north. Judah, Issachar, and Zebulun were to the east; Reuben, Simeon, and Gad were to the south; Ephraim, Manasseh, and Benjamin were to the west; and Dan, Asher, and Naphtali were to the north. They were trained to be orderly and balanced is setting up camp.

> And the children of Israel did according to all that the Lord commanded Moses: so they pitched by their standards, and so they set forward, every one after their families, according to the house of their fathers (Numbers 2:34).

In Numbers 3 Moses gave specific instructions about the duties of the Levites. Just as they were specifically told where to pitch their tents and how to set up their camp, so they were given specific duties. Moses instructed them to operate always in an orderly fashion. We can apply this to our own lives: when our lives are orderly we have a sense of quietness and peace, and we can function properly.

NUMBERS 5
Guarding Against Infection

† † †

If a person is truly obedient to God, do you think there is any danger of his being infected?

It is the common thought that if a person's intentions are right, he is in no danger of being infected. But this is not true. The soul that trusts in God should take all precautions and then rest in God. A gardener who plans to raise beans knows that God will make them grow, but he needs to remember that the beans should be planted in a certain way according to their nature.

Israel obeyed God when they came out of Egypt; but the land which they entered was infected because of the people who had been there. Therefore, in Numbers 5 Moses taught Israel how to avoid infection. This is also important for us today, because each of us lives in the midst of an evil world. Around us all manner of conditions exist that would cause us to deteriorate by the very nature of the infection that we could receive. What we see, what we hear, and what we are active in all have in them the marks of human depravity. They crowd in upon us; there is no magical way we can avoid these things. Safety depends upon careful attention under the grace of God.

> Command the children of Israel, that they put out of the camp every leper, and every one that hath an issue, and whosoever is defiled by the dead: both male and female shall ye put out, without the camp shall ye put them; that they defile not their camps, in the midst whereof I dwell. And the children of Israel did so, and put them out without the camp (Numbers 5:2–4).

We need to read this with an open mind. There is no rebuke

or mistreatment of those who are infected even if they are causing infection; there is just precaution that it does not spread. Unless he has definite reasons according to God's Word, a believer cannot afford to socialize with a sinner who openly flaunts sin—openly using profanity, sharing in obscene jokes, or being generally immoral in relationships. Believers must be careful to immunize and sterilize themselves in all relations with people like that.

In verses 5 to 10 there is reference to an intimate matter concerning a man or woman who commits immorality. Moses directed that

> . . . they shall confess their sin which they have done: and he shall recompense his trespass with the principal thereof, and add unto it the fifth part thereof, and give it unto him against whom he hath trespassed (Numbers 5:7).

Restitution was to be given to a kinsman as to the Lord.

In verses 11 to 31 a long passage deals with something even more intimate. There is an elaborate description of the steps that had to be taken if a husband or wife trespassed by lying carnally with another man or woman. Something had to be done carefully to straighten these matters out. Apparently the social situation in which they lived was such that disease was common among the Canaanites, and promiscuous relationships with other people would increase the danger of disease. The danger of infection was so great that even the suspicion of infidelity was to be tested, through an elaborate process.

Today pure food laws are rigidly enforced by our government, with severe penalty for infringements, and we consider ourselves advanced in the prevention of disease. Yet we permit pornography. We not only permit it over the news media, but we tolerate novels and TV shows that are obscene. Sinful people have always existed, but sin has not always been accepted. We are not living in the land of the Canaanites, but we too have to contend with people among us whose conduct could lead us directly into sin.

Moses would have warned and guarded against all sinful behavior by exercising the procedures of quarantine, isolation, and vaccinations. It is easier to prevent sin and disease than to rid ourselves of it.

NUMBERS 6
Law for the Nazarite

† † †

Do you think it could be helpful for a believer to set special seasons of unusual commitment to God in his conduct?

Every now and then certain believers appear who act in a special way for religious reasons. One of the most easily noticed differences is the matter of dress. For example, it is the custom among some for the men never to wear a tie and among others for the women to wear no jewelry. There are also people who make it a rule to fast for a specified time for religious reasons.

Numbers 6 draws attention to such practices among the people back in the days of the exodus of Israel. Moses outlined instructions to guide people who made vows. Among them were individuals who adopted what they called a Nazarite vow, which was apparently for a limited time. The essential element in this Nazarite vow seemed to be a negative restriction in terms of what the person could not eat and what he could not do. We read:

> And the Lord spake unto Moses, saying, Speak unto the children of Israel, and say unto them, When either man or woman shall separate themselves to vow a vow of a Nazarite, to separate themselves unto the Lord: he shall separate himself from wine and strong drink, and shall drink no vinegar of wine, or vinegar of strong drink, neither shall he drink any liquor of grapes, nor eat moist grapes, or dried. All the days of his separation shall he eat nothing that is made of the vine tree, from the kernels even to the husk. All the days of the vow of his separation there shall no razor come upon his head: until the days be fulfilled, in the which, he separateth himself unto the Lord, he shall be holy, and shall let the locks of the hair of his head grow. All the days that he separateth himself unto the

> Lord he shall come at no dead body. He shall not make himself
> unclean for his father, or for his mother, for his brother, or for
> his sister, when they die: because the consecration of his God is
> upon his head. All the days of his separation he is holy unto the
> Lord (Numbers 6:1–8).

A man who made a vow of this sort set himself aside in a special way by his conduct. He was to keep his vow absolutely, even refusing to do things that would ordinarily be expected of him.

Verses 9–11 describe how the man should cleanse himself if he happened to be in the presence of someone who died; for the presence of death "defiled the head of his consecration."

These were specific instructions which spoke of how he should carry through his commitment to separate himself entirely as unto the Lord. Things of the Lord were even to be above matters of his own family.

Moses outlined specific instructions with careful procedures. The man was to follow this special procedure even if he couldn't have prevented his defilement. Verses 13 to 21 set forth a careful procedure for the Nazarite to follow when he returned to live with the rest of the congregation.

If you know someone who dresses in a special way and who adopts certain other procedures for religious reasons, are you tempted to scorn him? When I was a young believer in Christ I had a negative attitude toward anybody who put on a robe to preach in a pulpit or to sing in a choir. However, different people believe in different distinctive practices to enhance their worship of God, and we should accept them on this basis.

Toward the latter part of this chapter we find one of the most wonderful passages in all Scripture. Today we call that the Aaronic Blessing, and we still use this beautiful prayer in worship, usually as a benediction:

> The Lord bless thee, and keep thee: the Lord make his face
> shine upon thee, and be gracious unto thee: the Lord lift up his
> countenance upon thee, and give thee peace (Numbers
> 6:24–26).

NUMBERS 7

Leading the People

† † †

Did you know that the spiritual service of the leaders of a congregation has much to do with the way God blesses the people as a whole?

Anytime a group of people gets together, the group needs leaders in order to exist in any kind of order. But anyone who wants to lead must serve the common people. Jesus taught this:

> Ye know that the princes of the Gentiles exercise dominion over them, and they that are great exercise authority upon them. But it shall not be so among you: but whosoever will be great among you, let him be your minister: and whosoever will be chief among you, let him be your servant: even as the Son of man came not to be ministered unto, but to minister, and to give his life a ransom for many (Matthew 20:25–28).

And in Luke 22:27 He made the statement: "I am among you as he that serveth."

In a situation where a number live together, somebody is usually in charge. Others often look up to him and ascribe to him all the honor of his position. Soon they begin to think he is someone unique. Even if they do not think so, he is inclined to think so. But that is not the way it was in Moses' plan from God. God gave Moses extensive instructions to guide the leaders of Israel as to how they were to serve the people.

> And it came to pass on that day the Moses had fully set up the tabernacle, and had anointed it, and sanctified it, and all the instruments thereof, both the altar and all the vessels thereof, and had anointed them, and sanctified them; that the princes of Israel, heads of the house of their fathers, who were the princes of the tribes, and were over them that were numbered, of-

> fered: and they brought their offering before the Lord, six
> covered wagons, and twelve oxen; a wagon for two of the
> princes, and for each one an ox: and they brought them before
> the tabernacle. And the Lord spake unto Moses, saying, Take it
> of them, that they may be to do the service of the tabernacle of
> the congregation (Numbers 7:1–5).

The life of the people of Israel was led by these leaders. All
the people were to come before God, the leaders coming first
and making the offering in order that the work of the tabernacle might be carried on.

> And thou shalt give them unto the Levites, to every man ac-
> cording to his service. And Moses took the wagons and the
> oxen, and gave them unto the Levites. Two wagons and four
> oxen he gave unto the sons of Gershon, according to their
> service: and four wagons and eight oxen he gave unto the sons
> of Merari, according unto their service, under the hand of
> Ithamar the son of Aaron the priest. But unto the sons of
> Kohath he gave none: because the service of the sanctuary
> belonging unto them was that they should bear upon their
> shoulders (Number 7:5–9).

When it came to the distribution of the offering or the re-
sources to the workers, distinctions were made. Not everyone
got the same, but each received according to his service.

Next followed an interesting account about all the various
princes, offering from the various tribes in a most astonishing
manner. Numbers 7:12–83 reports the record of what all the
tribes, through their representatives (princes), brought as offerings. Although all twelve are detailed in succession, they
are all the same, offered the same way.

When a believer comes into the church service he may
think he is just one of hundreds. But this is not the way God
thinks. The worshiper is one of one to God, regardless of who
he is. The Lord personally receives service from each individual. There is one obvious lesson here: the leaders are to
offer, but each individual is to do his part. And in verses 84 to
88 we have a careful record of what was offered for the dedication of the altar. When we think about the altar in the tabernacle, it should remind us of Calvary's cross. The altar is
where the sacrifice was made by the priest; the cross is where
the sacrifice was made by the Lord. Because of this, the
center of all worship is the altar forever.

And when Moses was gone into the tabernacle of the congregation to speak with him, then he heard the voice of one speaking unto him from off the mercy seat that was upon the ark of testimony, from between the two cherubim: and he spake unto him (Numbers 7:89).

When the offerings are made and the service proceeds as God desires it to, we actually have communication with the almighty God, who reveals His will to His servants. We talk to God, and He talks to us; this is what the worship of God is all about.

NUMBERS 8
Presenting the Levites

† † †

Can you understand that in the arranging of facilities for congregational worship, a crew of persons must work at it daily?

Christians can expect blessings from God in their daily living according to their faith. But not everyone realizes that faith must be nurtured. We do not always have the same amount of faith so we nurture it through worship services. Peter wrote, "Desire the sincere milk of the word, that ye might grow thereby" (1 Peter 2:2).

In order to promote religious activities we must have a crew of workers, whom we speak of as elders, deacons, teachers, and so on. In the time of early Israel one tribe, Levi, was set aside for this service. The Levites' duties were to serve the people in promoting worship, teaching, communing, and various other activities that strengthened their relationship with God.

The Levites were given no land in Canaan. When Joshua supervised the partitioning of the land as the Israelites entered Canaan, he gave a portion to each of the twelve tribes, including both tribes of Joseph: Ephraim and Manasseh. But he gave none to the Levites, because they would be too preoccupied with their service in the tabernacle to work the land, and they would live off the tithes the people brought to the priest.

In Numbers 8, the function of the Levites is described:

> And the Lord spake unto Moses, saying, Speak unto Aaron, and say unto him, when thou lightest the lamps, the seven lamps shall give light over against the candlestick (Numbers 8:1-2).

This emphasizes that what will follow has to do with the giving of light. This immediately brings to our attention the purpose of the Levites: to shed light among the people.

> And Aaron did so; he lighted the lamps thereof over against the candlestick, as the Lord commanded Moses. . . .
>
> And the Lord spake unto Moses, saying, Take the Levites from among the children of Israel, and cleanse them. And thus shalt thou do unto them, to cleanse them: Sprinkle water of purifying upon them, and let them shave all their flesh, and let them wash their clothes, and so make themselves clean (Numbers 8:3, 5–7).

It is very important that a person who is to serve the Lord, especially as a leader, should be cleansed of all sin.

> Then let them take a young bullock with his meat offering, even fine flour mingled with oil, and another young bullock shalt thou take for a sin offering. And thou shalt bring the Levites before the Lord: and the children of Israel shall put their hands upon the Levites: and Aaron shall offer the Levites before the Lord for an offering of the children of Israel, that they may execute the service of the Lord (Numbers 8:8, 10–11).

This gesture of putting their hands upon the Levites was a matter of the congregation of people committing the responsibility of their experience and their lives to the Levites. The Levites were then to shave their hair, wash their clothes and make themselves clean.

The Levites were to be offered to the Lord as a sacrifice on behalf of the people. That is a proper understanding of the relationship the leaders of Israel, and the leaders of the church in our day, have with God, who will deal with them.

> And the Levites shall lay their hands upon the heads of the bullocks: and thou shalt offer the one for a sin offering, and the other for a burnt offering, unto the Lord, to make an atonement for the Levites (Numbers 8:12).

The Levites were to go through a ritual that would indicate that they were confessing their sins and would be cleansed, committing themselves whole-heartedly to the service of the Lord. Their acceptability to the Lord was on the basis of their sacrifices, not on an examination. The whole question was whether or not they were committed. They were to be committed to God in this sacrament of offering. They simply transferred their responsibility to the sacrifice, which we now know represented Christ Jesus.

> And thou shalt set the Levites before Aaron, and before his sons, and offer them for an offering unto the Lord. Thus shalt thou separate the Levites from among the children of Israel: and the Levites shall be mine. And after that shall the Levites go in to do the service of the tabernacle of the congregation: and thou shalt cleanse them, and offer them for an offering (Numbers 8:13–15).

We should not miss the phrase "after that." After they had been dedicated, cleansed, and committed to do the will of God, then they could go in and do the work that was set aside for them. We read in this chapter that the Levites were given as a gift to the Lord to serve Him in place of the firstborn. All of this was done that Israel might be blessed by God. In the same way the people who must serve the Lord in this special way today are our church workers.

This chapter also contains instruction for leaders. After confessing their sins and being cleansed, they were to offer themselves in order to bring the people closer to God, just as the Levites were to serve as representatives of the Lord by the grace of God.

NUMBERS 9

Passover

† † †

Do you realize that the Christian is not responsible to decide for himself which daily course of action will most likely be wise and good, but he is responsible to obey conscientiously what he understands God wants him to do?

When the children of Israel had been brought out of Egypt by the goodness and power of God, Moses told them what God wanted them to do to make sure they would remember Him. He didn't want His acts to become ordinary to them. At the Red Sea Israel had been delivered from the power of Egypt, so that they were free to journey to Canaan. But they were not so free that they could direct their own steps. The almighty God led Moses to guide them by establishing certain times in their calendar when they would remember God especially. God would always be their refuge and their stronghold, but they needed to remember this in a special way.

Moses instructed Israel about God's part in their affairs, by instituting the Passover Feast. Before they came out of Egypt there was the special occasion when God passed over them on the last great plague: the death of the firstborn. God had then given, through Moses, instructions that they should remember this event with an annual feast called the Passover.

And the Lord spake unto Moses in the wilderness of Sinai, in the first month of the second year after they were come out of the land of Egypt, saying, Let the children of Israel also keep the passover at his appointed season. In the fourteenth day of this month, at even, ye shall keep it in his appointed season: according to all the rites of it, and according to all the ceremonies thereof, shall ye keep it. And Moses spake unto the children of Israel, that they should keep the passover. And

> they kept the passover on the fourteenth day of the first month
> at even in the wilderness of Sinai: according to all that the Lord
> commanded Moses, so did the children of Israel (Numbers
> 9:1–5).

The people were to take special care in the way they practiced this ceremony. They were to be clean in their relationship with God. It was possible for them to become unclean and defiled by such things as the dead body of a man and thus not be able to keep the Passover on that day.

> And those men said unto him, We are defiled by the dead body
> of a man: wherefore are we kept back, that we may not offer an
> offering of the Lord in his appointed season among the children
> of Israel? And Moses said unto them, Stand still, and I will hear
> what the Lord will command concerning you (Numbers 9:7–8).

In verses 9 to 14 special procedures were authorized for them, making it clear that all must share in this celebration.

The sacrament of the Lord's Supper should be celebrated in the life of all believers in Christ. This is the way believers remember that their whole relationship with God is based upon Christ's death for them. The truth is that believers serve God not because He is so good, nor because they are so virtuous, but because Christ died for them.

> And if a stranger shall sojourn among you, and will keep the
> passover unto the Lord; according to the ordinance of the pass-
> over, and according to the manner thereof, so shall he do: ye
> shall have one ordinance, both for the stranger, and for him
> that was born in the land (Numbers 9:14).

When the Passover took place in Egypt the Hebrews were all primed to move, and so in this chapter, after noting that all were to celebrate the Passover, instructions were again given to go forward.

> And on the day that the tabernacle was reared up the cloud
> covered the tabernacle namely, the tent of the testimony: and
> at even there was upon the tabernacle as it were the appear-
> ance of fire, until the morning. So it was alway: the cloud
> covered it by day, and the appearance of fire by night. And
> when the cloud was taken up from the tabernacle, then after
> that the children of Israel journeyed: and in the place where
> the cloud abode, there the children of Israel pitched their
> tents. At the commandment of the Lord the children of Israel
> journeyed, and at the commandment of the Lord they pitched:

as long as the cloud abode upon the tabernacle they rested in their tents. And when the cloud tarried long upon the tabernacle many days, then the children of Israel kept the charge of the Lord, and journeyed not. And so it was, when the cloud was a few days upon the tabernacle; according to the commandment of the Lord they abode in their tents, and according to the commandment of the Lord they journeyed. And so it was, when the cloud abode from even unto the morning, and that the cloud was taken up in the morning, then they journeyed: whether it was by day or by night that the cloud was taken up, they journeyed (Numbers 9:15–21).

Whether it was a month or a year that the cloud tarried upon the tabernacle, the children of Israel remained for that length of time; but when the cloud was lifted, they journeyed. The parallel for believers today is that we want His presence with us all of the time. Christ gave Himself for us, He bought us, and we belong to Him. The children of Israel were disciplined in this matter: they moved only when God wanted them to move, and they stood still when He wanted them to stand still. When the cloud moved, they moved. This indicates that God was showing His moment by moment attention to His people, and they were walking with Him.

NUMBERS 10
On the March

† † †

Can you understand that all preparation of the people of God for living must eventually lead to action?

It is unfortunate that for many the matter of belonging to the Lord, or even living a spiritual life, is largely a matter of the mind. These believers encourage each other to think on the things of God and then spend some time talking with each other about what they think. Often they spell out their ideas and put them into words, make up doctrines, and make up explanations. Thus they get theologies and points of view, which they compare and discuss, imagining that they are worshiping God and performing something in His name when they talk and talk.

Doubtless the truth of God comes to the heart through the mind. The truth of God comes by His Word which is addressed to the hearing, and thus gets into the mind. But it is a grievous error if all that believers do with reference to their ideas of God and their relationship with Him is argue about opinions. The truth is much more than that.

Both the reconciling of people to God by the Lord Jesus Christ and the giving of the Holy Spirit into their hearts to comfort them and to guide them must eventuate in action. We need to pay attention to the message of James that faith without works is dead. We must put our ideas into practice.

It is important that Israel took time out to learn what the Word of God was. Moses went up to the mount and received the Ten Words, afterwards explaining them to the people. And Israel had the plan of the camp and the tabernacle, which showed them how to come to worship God. All those things were important, but they were incidental to the journey. Israel was to move.

Numbers 10 gives instructive detail about how Israel was to be guided on the march.

> Make thee two trumpets of silver; of a whole piece shalt thou make them: that thou mayest use them for the calling of the assembly, and for the journeying of the camps. And when they shall blow with them, all the assembly shall assemble themselves to thee at the door of the tabernacle of the congregation (Number 10:2–3).

Today our preachers and teachers, like those silver trumpets, gather the people together and lead them along the way. They lead our spiritual thinking, and they interpret the Word of God for us.

> And when they shall blow with them, all the assembly shall assemble themselves to thee at the door of the tabernacle of the congregation. And if they blow but with one trumpet, then the princes, which are heads of the thousands of Israel, shall gather themselves unto thee. When ye blow an alarm, then the camps that lie on the east parts shall go forward. When ye blow an alarm the second time, then the camps that lie on the south side shall take their journey: they shall blow an alarm for their journeys. But when the congregation is to be gathered together, ye shall blow, but ye shall not sound an alarm. And the sons of Aaron, the priests, shall blow with the trumpets; and they shall be to you for an ordinance for ever throughout your generations (Numbers 10:3–8).

We need to be called together to worship, that we may draw nigh unto Him. We need leaders to challenge us to go forward into action under the careful guidance of the almighty God.

> And if ye go to war in your land against the enemy that oppresseth you, then ye shall blow an alarm with the trumpets; and ye shall be remembered before the Lord your God, and ye shall be saved from your enemies (Numbers 10:9).

Certain things need to be done by believers together, not individually. Believers need to stand with others and heed the voice of the Lord that they may share in the triumphal victory He will give to them.

> Also in the day of your gladness, and in your solemn days, and in the beginnings of your months, ye shall blow with the trumpets over your burnt offerings, and over the sacrifices of your

peace offerings; that they may be to you for a memorial before
your God: I am the Lord your God (Numbers 10:10).

The Lord is our God; believers need to be reminded to take
this to heart. The preacher must rise up before us, sound the
trumpet, and tell us what God would have us to do.

> And it came to pass on the twentieth day of the second month,
> in the second year, that the cloud was taken up from off the
> tabernacle of the testimony. And the children of Israel took
> their journeys out of the wilderness of Sinai; and the cloud
> rested in the wilderness of Paran. And they first took their
> journey according to the commandment of the Lord by the
> hand of Moses (Numbers 10:11–13).

NUMBERS 11
Complaining

† † †

Have you ever considered that complaining about the circumstances of daily living is actually a criticism of God?

When a person believes there is one God, and that the almighty God is sovereign, he can understand that God either causes or allows all situations to be the way they are. Therefore, when a person is dissatisfied with his lot and complains, he is actually charging God with not ruling his life properly. This is a broad statement, but it is true.

> And when the people complained, it displeased the Lord: and the Lord heard it; and his anger was kindled; and the fire of the Lord burnt among them, and consumed them that were in the uttermost parts of the camp. And the people cried unto Moses; and when Moses prayed unto the Lord, the fire was quenched. And he called the name of the place Taberah: because the fire of the Lord burnt among them (Number 11:1–3).

This is a simple record, but it presents the whole picture.

> And the mixed multitude that was among them fell a-lusting: and the children of Israel also wept again, and said, Who shall give us flesh to eat (Numbers 11:4)?

When the Israelites left Egypt, a number of Egyptians came along. They were called a mixed multitude. In the desert some natural desires of these Egyptians came to the forefront.

> We remember the fish, which we did eat in Egypt freely: the cucumbers, and the melons, and the leeks, and the onions, and the garlic: but now our soul is dried away: there is nothing at all, beside this manna, before our eyes (Numbers 11:5–6).

They had been eating the manna, but after a time it became tasteless.

> And the manna was as coriander seed, and the color thereof as the color of bdellium. And the people went about, and gathered it, and ground it in mills, or beat it in a mortar, and baked it in pans, and made cakes of it: and the taste of it was as the taste of fresh oil. And when the dew fell upon the camp in the night, the manna fell upon it. Then Moses heard the people weep throughout their families, every man in the door of his tent: and the anger of the Lord was kindled greatly; Moses also was displeased (Numbers 11:7–10).

Complaints are a reflection upon the one who is responsible. If the almighty God is responsible and people complain, they are casting aspersions upon Him. For this reason, Israel's complaining distressed Moses.

> And Moses said unto the Lord, Wherefore hast thou afflicted thy servant? and wherefore have I not found favor in thy sight, that thou layest the burden of all this people upon me? Have I conceived all this people? have I begotten them, that thou shouldest say unto me, Carry them in thy bosom, as a nursing father beareth the sucking child, unto the land which thou swarest unto their fathers? Whence should I have flesh to give unto all this people? for they weep unto me, saying, Give us flesh, that we may eat. I am not able to bear all this people alone, because it is too heavy for me. And if thou deal thus with me, kill me, I pray thee, out of hand, if I have found favor in thy sight; and let me not see my wretchedness (Numbers 11:11–15).

This is the one time in his life when we find Moses complaining about the hand of God. Moses found it hard to accept his duty there.

Instead of rebuking Moses for the complaint, the Lord said unto Moses:

> . . . Gather unto me seventy men of the elders of Israel, whom thou knowest to be the elders of the people, and officers over them; and bring them unto the tabernacle of the congregation, that they may stand there with thee. And I will come down and talk with thee there: and I will take of the spirit which is upon thee, and will put it upon them; and they shall bear the burden of the people with thee, that thou bear it not thyself alone (Numbers 11:16–17).

When tasks are extremely difficult, it is always possible to make some adjustment. In this case, the solution was to let others share the responsibility.

And say thou unto the people, Sanctify yourselves against tomorrow, and ye shall eat flesh . . . (Numbers 11:18).

Moses found this hard to believe, because they were out in
the desert—far from any known source of supply of flesh.

> And Moses said, The people, among whom I am, are six hun-
> dred thousand footmen; and thou hast said, I will give them
> flesh, that they may eat a whole month. Shall the flocks and the
> herds be slain for them, to suffice them? or shall all the fish of
> the sea be gathered together for them, to suffice them? And the
> Lord said unto Moses, Is the Lord's hand waxed short? thou
> shalt see now whether my word shall come to pass unto thee or
> not. And Moses went out, and told the people the words of the
> Lord, and gathered the seventy men of the elders of the
> people, and set them round about the tabernacle. And the
> Lord came down in a cloud, and spake unto him, and took of
> the spirit that was upon him, and gave it unto the seventy
> elders: and it came to pass, that, when the spirit rested upon
> them, they prophesied, and did not cease. But there remained
> two of the men in the camp, the name of the one was Eldad,
> and the name of the other Medad: and the spirit rested upon
> them; and they were of them that were written, but went not
> out unto the tabernacle: and they prophesied in the camp. And
> there ran a young man, and told Moses, and said, Eldad and
> Medad do prophesy in the camp. And Joshua the son of Nun,
> the servant of Moses, one of his young men, answered and
> said, My lord Moses, forbid them. And Moses said unto him,
> Enviest thou for my sake? would God that all the Lord's people
> were prophets, and that the Lord would put his spirit upon
> them! And Moses gat him into the camp, he and the elders of
> Israel. And there went forth a wind from the Lord, and brought
> quails from the sea, and let them fall by the camp, as it were a
> day's journey on this side, and as it were a day's journey on the
> other side, round about the camp, and as it were two cubits
> high upon the face of the earth. And the people stood up all
> that day, and all that night, and all the next day, and they
> gathered the quails: he that gathered least gathered ten hom-
> ers: and they spread them all abroad for themselves round
> about the camp. And while the flesh was yet between their
> teeth, ere it was chewed, the wrath of the Lord was kindled
> against the people, and the Lord smote the people with a very
> great plague (Numbers 11:21–33).

Sometimes in our complaining, we get just what we insist
upon and suffer because of it. That is very sobering. We have
seen here in Numbers that the almighty God watches over
His people. There is much trouble in this world. But God's

hand is upon His people for good. In Corinthians we read how Paul said God will not suffer us to be tempted above that which we are able to bear. But with the temptation he will provide a way of escape. By the grace of God, believers look up to Him and ask for guidance, blessing, and strength to accept the situation as it is.

NUMBERS 12
Jealousy

† † †

Is it hard to believe that people who are committed to serving Christ in a responsible manner can be jealous of one another?

Much of the trouble we human beings have arises in the development of our "ego." We use the word "ego" to refer to the "I" element: I want this; I want to do that; I like this; I do not like that; I will go here; I will not go there. The ego is in a person from the time he is born. Babies have it: they want everything for themselves. A baby reaches out for anything he can get. If anyone tries to get anything away from him, no matter what it is, he will hang on for dear life. That is part of the evidence of sinfulness of our human nature.

When we get older we are conscious of this, but we still do it. It is natural to be sensitive about anything that seems to belittle or to ignore our egos. If people do not pay attention to us, we do not like them. In any given relationship with others, regardless of whether it is in the family, office, school or church, we tend to care especially about anything that affects us. No matter what is going on, if it does not affect us, we can forget it.

We shall see that this is the way in which servants of God, because they are human beings, can actually experience jealousy toward one another. Finer people than Moses, Aaron, and their sister Miriam are not to be found anywhere. But—

> Miriam and Aaron spake against Moses because of the Ethiopian woman whom he had married (Numbers 12:1).

In talking against Moses, they probably pointed out some fault. But the next verse gives a clue to the real reason they spoke against him.

> And they said, Hath the Lord indeed spoken only by Moses?
> hath he not spoken also by us? And the Lord heard it (Numbers
> 12:2).

The Lord was aware of their criticism of Moses.

> (Now the man Moses was very meek, above all the men which
> were upon the face of the earth.) And the Lord spake suddenly
> unto Moses, and unto Aaron, and unto Miriam, Come out ye
> three unto the tabernacle of the congregation. And they three
> came out. And the Lord came down in the pillar of the cloud,
> and stood in the door of the tabernacle, and called Aaron and
> Miriam: and they both came forth. And he said, Hear now my
> words: If there be a prophet among you, I the Lord will make
> myself known unto him in a vision, and will speak unto him in a
> dream (Numbers 12:3-6).

And then, of course, the prophet would interpret that dream and tell it to the people.

> My servant Moses is not so, who is faithful in all mine house.
> With him will I speak mouth to mouth, even apparently, and
> not in dark speeches; and the similtude of the Lord shall he
> behold: wherefore then were ye not afraid to speak against my
> servant Moses? And the anger of the Lord was kindled against
> them; and he departed (Numbers 12:7-9).

God takes note of criticism among His servants. If I in my heart allow some unjust criticism of a brother to arise, it will not go unnoticed by the Lord. Being jealous of Moses' authority, Miriam and Aaron criticized him about a social matter, which was not really the issue. Moses was very meek above all other men, and this meekness helps us to understand the attitude exemplified in Jesus of Nazareth. "Who, when he was reviled, reviled not again; when he suffered, he threatened not" (1 Peter 2:23). And this is very important to notice: Moses made no defense. Moses did not have the Holy Spirit helping him from within as we do, but he was a great servant of God. This is what a servant of God should do: be silent in the face of criticism.

When Moses did not reply, God did. He called for a show-down, illustrating Isaiah's reference to God's way of watching over His servants.

> No weapon that is formed against thee shall prosper; and every
> tongue that shall rise against thee in judgment thou shalt con-

demn. This is the heritage of the servants of the Lord, and their
righteousness is of me, saith the Lord (Isaiah 54:17).

This verse became important to me when I was the pastor of a
church and my work was criticized from time to time. I did
not feel too sure of myself, because I had made some blunders
and left some tasks undone. I copied this verse and put it in
the drawer of my desk at the office, so that when I pulled out
the drawer it lay before me. When I received a critical phone
call, that verse would bring me encouragement.

During Moses' time of trials the Lord came down and called
Miriam and Aaron out for a showdown. He pointed out to
them that sometimes He revealed His will to a prophet in a
vision or dream, but that with Moses He spoke plainly.
Moses, as His servant, was faithful in all His house. With him
the Lord did not speak in dark speeches. "And the similitude
of the Lord shall he behold: wherefore then were ye not afraid
to speak against my servant Moses?" Because God counted
Moses as His servant, it was dangerous for anyone to criticize
him. "And the anger of the Lord was kindled against them;
and he departed."

What happened then? It is a very simple story: Miriam was
stricken with leprosy.

. . . Behold, Miriam became leprous, white as snow: and
Aaron looked upon Miriam, and, behold, she was leprous
(Numbers 12:10).

What did they do then? It comes as no surprise that Aaron
said unto Moses,

. . . Alas, my lord, I beseech thee, lay not the sin upon us,
wherein we have done foolishly, and wherein we have sinned
(Numbers 12:11).

Moses had not accused them; God had. Working through
their consciences, working by His Spirit upon them, He
brought them to this. So Aaron asked Moses:

Let her not be as one dead, of whom the flesh is half consumed
when he cometh out of his mother's womb. And Moses cried
unto the Lord, saying, Heal her now, O God, I beseech thee.
And the Lord said unto Moses, If her father had but spit in her
face, should she not be ashamed seven days? let her be shut out
from the camp seven days, and after that let her be received in
again (Numbers 12:12–14).

She was healed immediately.

> And Miriam was shut out from the camp seven days: and the
> people journeyed not till Miriam was brought in again (Num-
> bers 12:15).

It is important to remember that as long as there is jealousy
between the leaders, the people will not make progress.

NUMBERS 13–14
Sending Out Spies

† † †

Wouldn't you think that if a believer wanted to do the Lord's will he should make a careful study of any project he was going into before he started it?

The lives of all of us are marked by times of planning. We try to find out everything we can about the situation so that we can have a grasp of the problem we are facing. Then we project possible options to enable us to make a good choice. This is a sensible, intelligent procedure which Jesus of Nazareth recommended.

> For which of you, intending to build a tower, sitteth not down first, and counteth the cost, whether he have sufficient to finish it (Luke 14:28)?

We need to keep this in mind as we think about walking in the Lord by faith. But sometimes, in spite of all plans, a procedure fails as it did in Numbers.

Israel had come to the point in their journey when entrance to Canaan was possible. This occurred about two years after they had left Egypt. At this time they were at Kadesh-barnea, where they would not have had to cross the river Jordan. They would have come to Canaan on the land side, the western side of Jordan.

> And the Lord spake unto Moses, saying, Send thou men, that they may search the land of Canaan, which I give unto the children of Israel: of every tribe of their fathers shall ye send a man, every one a ruler among them. And Moses by the commandment of the Lord sent them from the wilderness of Paran: all those men were heads of the children of Israel (Numbers 13:1–3).

Our report would have been that he sent out spies.

> And Moses sent them to spy out the land of Canaan, and said
> unto them, Get you up this way southward, and go up into the
> mountain: and see the land, what it is; and the people that
> dwelleth therein, whether they be strong or weak, few or
> many; and what the land is that they dwell in, whether it be
> good or bad; and what cities they be that they dwell in,
> whether in tents, or in strongholds; and what the land is,
> whether it be fat or lean, whether there be wood therein, or
> not. And be ye of good courage, and bring of the fruit of the
> land. Now the time was the time of the first ripe grapes. So
> they went up, and searched the land from the wilderness of Zin
> unto Rehob, as men come to Hamath . . . And they came unto
> the brook of Eshcol, and cut down from thence a branch with
> one cluster of grapes, and they bare it between two upon a
> staff; and they brought of the pomegranates, and of the figs . . .
> And they returned from searching of the land after forty days.
> And they went and came to Moses, and to Aaron, and to all the
> congregation of the children of Israel, unto the wilderness of
> Paran, to Kadesh; and brought back word unto them, and unto
> all the congregation, and showed them the fruit of the land
> (Numbers 13:17–26).

The fruit was so bountiful that it took two men to carry the
grapes of one vine. So the spies gave their report, and we read
further:

> . . . We came unto the land whither thou sentest us, and surely
> it floweth with milk and honey; and this is the fruit of it.
> Nevertheless the people be strong that dwell in the land, and
> the cities are walled, and very great: and moreover we saw the
> children of Anak there . . . And Caleb stilled the people before
> Moses, and said, Let us go up at once, and possess it; for we are
> well able to overcome it. But the men that went up with him
> said, We be not able to go up against the people; for they are
> stronger than we (Numbers 13:27–31).

Twelve men had been sent, and ten said Israel would not be
able to go against the inhabitants.

> And they brought up an evil report of the land which they had
> searched . . . And there we saw the giants, the sons of Anak,
> which come of the giants: and we were in our own sight as
> grasshoppers, and so we were in their sight. And all the
> congregation lifted up their voice, and cried; and the people
> wept that night. And all the children of Israel murmured
> against Moses and against Aaron (Numbers 13:32–14:2).

This is the record of how Israel made their great mistake.

. . . And the whole congregation said unto them, Would God that we had died in the land of Egypt! or would God we had died in this wilderness! And wherefore hath the Lord brought us unto this land, to fall by the sword, that our wives and our children should be a prey? were it not better for us to return into Egypt? And they said one to another, Let us make a captain, and let us return into Egypt (Numbers 14:2–4).

Just at the point where they could have taken action, they lost their confidence. They now wanted to turn back.

Joshua and Caleb tried to arouse the people:

Only rebel not ye against the Lord, neither fear ye the people of the land; for they are bread for us: their defense is departed from them, and the Lord is with us: fear them not. But all the congregation bade stone them with stones (Numbers 14:9–10).

So Israel rejected this advice. Joshua and Caleb knew that the cities were high walled and the soldiers were giants in the land, but they said that God would fight for them. They knew that, if God was for them, no one of consequence could be against them.

While this was going on, the Lord proposed to Moses that He would disinherit the people and make out of Moses a great nation that would obey Him. But Moses interceded for Israel. He argued that it would be to the glory of God to bring these people in. He said that if God did not bring Israel in, everybody would say He was not able to do it. Moses included in his argument:

The Lord is long-suffering, and of great mercy, forgiving iniquity and transgression, and by no means clearing the guilty, visiting the iniquity of the fathers upon the children unto the third and fourth generation. Pardon, I beseech thee, the iniquity of this people according unto the greatness of thy mercy, and as thou hast forgiven this people, from Egypt even until now (Numbers 14:18–19).

God heard Moses and granted his request:

And the Lord said, I have pardoned according to thy word: but as truly as I live, all the earth shall be filled with the glory of the Lord. Because all those men . . . have not hearkened to my voice; surely they shall not see the land which I sware unto their fathers . . . but my servant Caleb . . . him will I bring into the land whereinto he went. . . . Tomorrow turn you, and get you into the wilderness (Numbers 14:20–25).

Moses reported the mind of God to the people and told them that that generation would never go into the land. They had not wanted to go forward because they were afraid to, but they did not want to go back because they hated to. There is a marvelous truth here that should be noted: if the time comes to go forward with the Lord and the believer does not go forward because he doubts, he must go backward. He cannot stand still.

In willful arrogance the people decided to go in anyway, even though Moses warned them not to. He told them the Lord would not be with them. But they went, and they were defeated. As illustrated in this example, failure to move forward in obedience means retreat into the past.

NUMBERS 15
Sacrifices

† † †

Can you see the importance of taking care to remember God in every event in life?

The old saying "Out of sight, out of mind" is often true. Because we do not see God, it is easy to forget Him. And that is dangerous. Those who know about the gospel and who believe in the Lord Jesus Christ live by faith. But that confidence in Him fluctuates. Today I can feel closer, and tomorrow I may feel further away. Today the things of the Lord may be dim in my mind; tomorrow they may be clear.

Moses knew that the people of Israel were just human beings, who were prone to forget God. So Moses gave them special instructions to help them keep God in mind.

> Speak unto the children of Israel, and say unto them, When ye be come into the land of your habitations, which I give unto you, and will make an offering by fire unto the Lord, a burnt offering, or a sacrifice in performing a vow, or in a freewill offering, or in your solemn feasts, to make a sweet savor unto the Lord, of the herd, or of the flock: then shall he that offereth his offering unto the Lord bring a meat offering of a tenth deal of flour mingled with the fourth part of a hin of oil (Numbers 15:2–4).

Moses detailed the possible offering they should bring. Whether it was a burnt offering, a freewill offering, a peace offering, or a meat offering, they often used oil and wine. It is common in studying Scripture to assume that oil symbolizes the function of the Holy Spirit, and wine symbolizes the death of Jesus—the pouring out of His blood. This implies that when they brought their offering to God they did so as they were led by the Holy Spirit, and on the basis of the fact that

the Messiah (the Christ) would die for them. It is meaningful
for us too, because ". . . these things happened unto them for
examples: and they are written for our admonition, upon
whom the ends of the world are come" (1 Corinthians 10:11).

Worshipers in Israel were to come before God repeatedly
and bring a burnt offering to indicate their desire to follow
Him totally, or a trespass offering to confess wrongdoing. We
also have certain ways of remembering. From the Scriptures
we have guidance to observe one day a week as the Lord's
Day, when we attend church and Bible classes. But we cannot
wait from Sunday to Sunday to turn to God or we will drift
away from Him. We must come to God daily in prayer. We
should pray for our family, for our church, and for others. This
will keep us closer to God than mere Sunday worship.

Moses gave them more specific guidance:

> And if a stranger sojourn with you, or whosoever be among you
> in your generations, and will offer an offering made by fire, of a
> sweet savor unto the Lord; as ye do, so he shall do. One law
> and one manner shall be for you, and for the stranger that
> sojourneth with you (Numbers 15:14, 16).

Have you ever had the experience of wondering what to do in
the matter of worshiping God when you have a visitor in your
home? Should you return thanks at the table? I hope you will.
Will you have Bible reading? By all means do so, so that your
visitor may be blessed by it. In Numbers 15:17–20 Moses told
the people to praise God whenever they ate: "When ye eat of
the bread of the land, ye shall offer up a heave offering."
Because the heave offering symbolized praise to the Lord, the
generalization of this command is to offer praise to the Lord at
mealtime. This is one reason that believing people customar-
ily offer thanks at meals.

Moses instructed them further, that if there should be sin
committed through ignorance in the congregation, all should
offer a burnt offering, which implied total dedication. The
priest was to make an atonement for all, and the sin would be
forgiven. The stranger was also to be in on this procedure.

> And if any soul sin through ignorance, then he shall bring a she
> goat of the first year for a sin offering. And the priest shall make
> an atonement for the soul that sinneth ignorantly . . . and it
> shall be forgiven him (Numbers 15:27–28).

This was common daily practice by which they sought to stay close to God. In the New Testament a different principle was followed because of Jesus Christ's great sacrifice, once and for all:

> If we confess our sins, he is faithful and just to forgive us our sins, and to cleanse us from all unrighteousness (1 John 1:9).

NUMBERS 16
Rebellion

† † †

Can you understand why dissatisfaction with the leaders of a congregation can be harmful?

The natural man does not like to be controlled. We see this in a baby and especially in a three-or four-year-old. It is particularly noticeable in a group if the one in control is a meek, humble person. The people under him oftentimes do not want to be told what to do. The history of Israel is marked by the notorious rebellion of Korah, a leader under Moses.

> Now Korah, the son of Izhar, the son of Kohath, the son of Levi, and Dathan and Abiram, the sons of Eliab, and On, the son of Peleth, sons of Reuben, took men: and they rose up before Moses, with certain of the children of Israel, two hundred and fifty princes of the assembly, famous in the congregation, men of renown: and they gathered themselves together against Moses and against Aaron, and said unto them, Ye take too much upon you, seeing all the congregation are holy, every one of them, and the Lord is among them: wherefore then lift ye up yourselves above the congregation of the Lord (Numbers 16:1–3)?

That is a typical complaint of those who are jealous of the leaders, because they assume that authority is a function of personal superiority. We know that in spiritual matters that is simply not true. Any man serving as a servant of God can speak authoritatively as from God. But here we see these people challenging Moses and Aaron, and Moses did not shrink from that challenge.

> And when Moses heard it, he fell upon his face: and he spake unto Korah and unto all his company, saying, Even tomorrow the Lord will show who are his, and who is holy; and will cause

100

him to come near unto him: even him whom he hath chosen
will he cause to come near unto him. This do; Take you censers, Korah, and all his company; and put fire therein, and put
incense in them before the Lord tomorrow: and it shall be that
the man whom the Lord doth choose, he shall be holy: ye take
too much upon you, ye sons of Levi (Numbers 16:4–7).

That was the very expression used in verse 3 when they said
to Moses and Aaron, "Ye take too much upon you."

And Moses said unto Korah, Hear, I pray you, ye sons of Levi:
seemeth it but a small thing unto you, that the God of Israel
hath separated you from the congregation of Israel, to bring
you near to himself to do the service of the tabernacle of the
Lord, and to stand before the congregation to minister unto
them (Numbers 16:8–9)?

In other words, "Don't you appreciate the responsibility you
have? Don't you recognize that you have been asked to be
leaders, with certain privileges because of this? And now you
are questioning the judgment of the leader chosen by God."

And Moses sent to call Dathan and Abiram, the sons of Eliab:
which said, We will not come up: is it a small thing that thou
hast brought us up out of a land that floweth with milk and
honey, to kill us in the wilderness, except thou make thyself
altogether a prince over us? Moreover thou hast not brought us
into a land that floweth with milk and honey, or given us inheritance of fields and vineyards: wilt thou put out the eyes of
these men? we will not come up (Numbers 16:12–14).

This refusal brought swift, stern action:

And Moses was very wroth, and said unto the Lord, Respect
not thou their offering: I have not taken one ass from them,
neither have I hurt one of them (Numbers 16:15).

It was said about Moses that he was the meekest man on the
face of the earth, yet when his authority in the Lord was
challenged, Moses was not in any way a mild man. He was
very firm, and he even asked God not to respect his accusers.

And Moses said unto Korah, Be thou and all thy company
before the Lord, thou, and they, and Aaron, tomorrow: and
take every man his censer, and put incense in them, and bring
ye before the Lord every man his censer, two hundred and fifty
censers; thou also, and Aaron, each of you his censer. And they
took every man his censer, and put fire in them, and laid
incense thereon, and stood in the door of the tabernacle of the

> congregation with Moses and Aaron. And Korah gathered all
> the congregation against them unto the door of the tabernacle
> of the congregation: and the glory of the Lord appeared unto all
> the congregation (Numbers 16:16–19).

God tested Moses and Aaron with the proposal that Israel be destroyed.

> And the Lord spake unto Moses and unto Aaron, saying, Sepa-
> rate yourselves from among this congregation, that I may con-
> sume them in a moment. And they fell upon their faces, and
> said, O God, the God of the spirits of all flesh, shall one man
> sin, and wilt thou be wroth with all the congregation? And the
> Lord spake unto Moses, saying, Speak unto the congregation,
> saying, Get you up from about the tabernacle of Korah,
> Dathan, and Abiram (Numbers 16:20–24).

Moses sent word to the people to get away from their tents and away from all those people who had rebelled against him, because God was going to show Israel something.

> And Moses said, Hereby ye shall know that the Lord hath sent
> me to do all these works; for I have not done them of mine own
> mind. If these men die the common death of all men, or if they
> be visited after the visitation of all men; then the Lord hath not
> sent me. But if the Lord make a new thing, and the earth open
> her mouth, and swallow them up, with all that appertain unto
> them, and they go down quick into the pit; then ye shall under-
> stand that these men have provoked the Lord (Numbers
> 16:28–30).

Moses took his stand right there and told them what was going to happen, and it did, exactly as he said.

> And all Israel that were round about them fled at the cry of
> them: for they said, Lest the earth swallow us up also (Num-
> bers 16:34).

> But on the morrow all the congregation of the children of Israel
> murmured against Moses and against Aaron, saying, Ye have
> killed the people of the Lord (Numbers 16:41).

Now God tested Moses and Aaron again, in threatening to destroy Israel.

> Get you up from among this congregation, that I may consume
> them as in a moment. And they fell upon their faces. And
> Moses said unto Aaron, Take a censer, and put fire therein
> from off the altar, and put on incense, and go quickly unto the
> congregation, and make an atonement for them: for there is

wrath gone out from the Lord; the plague is begun. And Aaron took as Moses commanded, and ran into the midst of the congregation; and, behold, the plague was begun among the people: and he put on incense, and made an atonement for the people. And he stood between the dead and the living; and the plague was stayed (Numbers 16:45–48).

In the course of all this, Moses and Aaron never lost sight of their responsibility to be the shepherds of the people. True, there was rebellion on the part of some of the leaders, and Moses dealt sternly with them. But when God suggested to Moses that He destroy all the people, Moses and Aaron ran out to make an atonement that the people might be spared.

In this particular case, Moses and Aaron represent the work that Christ Jesus does for us. And as we think about Numbers 16 we should watch carefully that we do not allow any kind of jealousy to come into our hearts about other leaders. If God sees fit to give other leaders responsibility over us, we should accept it quietly and not rebel against the leadership of those whom the Lord has chosen.

But if it should develop that in the course of this the whole company is threatened with disaster because of the foolishness of some rebel, then it is our responsibility to pray that the people may be spared the consequences of the foolishness of the rebel. We must remember that the almighty God is no weakling, and He will protect the man who is under Him when his authority is challenged. But we should never forget Moses and Aaron praying that the very people who criticized them should not be destroyed.

NUMBERS 17–18
Servants of the Lord

✝   ✝   ✝

Do you ever have any question as to whether ministers should live off the church offering?

It is easy for the layman to make the mistake of thinking the minister is imposing on his congregation by depending upon the church for his livelihood. There are even groups of Christians who pride themselves upon the fact that their ministers do not receive a salary, perhaps thinking this is a mark of special spirituality. But the Bible teaches that the servants of the Lord are to be provided for by the people whom they serve. We find this revealed in Numbers 17 and 18, where we find a plain outline of the arrangements that were made concerning the men who served by attending to the matters of religious exercises. These men were to be provided for by the people through their tithes. That was the reason why almighty God arranged for the people to turn over one tenth of their income to the Lord.

The tithe was not turned over to the Lord with the idea of piling up some big reserve fund; it was actually used for support. Somebody had to take care of the means of worship, and in those days the worship was elaborate. The Levites were to be without property, so that they could live off the tithe. Like any other group project, this required someone in authority: Aaron.

There had been trouble because of jealousy of Aaron; therefore, Numbers 17 and 18 reveal the will of God concerning the Levites. Each tribe was to select one person who would represent the tribe by taking a rod made of wood. The instructions were to

. . . write thou every man's name upon his rod. And thou shalt write Aaron's name upon the rod of Levi: for one rod shall be for the head of the house of their fathers. And thou shalt lay them up in the tabernacle of the congregation before the testimony, where I will meet with you. And it shall come to pass, that the man's rod, whom I shall choose, shall blossom: and I will make to cease from me the murmurings of the children of Israel, whereby they murmur against you (Numbers 17:2–5).

So they put these thirteen rods there before the Lord:

And Moses laid up the rods before the Lord in the tabernacle of witness. And it came to pass, that on the morrow Moses went into the tabernacle of witness; and, behold, the rod of Aaron for the house of Levi was budded, and brought forth buds, and bloomed blossoms, and yielded almonds.

And Moses brought out all the rods from before the Lord unto all the children of Israel: and they looked, and took every man his rod. And the Lord said unto Moses, Bring Aaron's rod again before the testimony, to be kept for a token against the rebels; and thou shalt quite take away their murmurings from me, that they die not (Numbers 17:7–10).

They took Aaron's rod and put it in the ark, the chest in the place of worship under the mercy seat. In that they put the tables of stone with the Ten Commandments on them and Aaron's rod that budded, which was forever to be evidence that Aaron was the one who was chosen:

And the Lord said unto Aaron, Thou and thy sons and thy father's house with thee shall bear the iniquity of the sanctuary: and thou and thy sons with thee shall bear the iniquity of your priesthood. And thy brethren also of the tribe of Levi, the tribe of thy father, bring thou with thee, that they may be joined unto thee, and minister unto thee: but thou and thy sons with thee shall minister before the tabernacle of witness. And they shall keep thy charge, and the charge of all the tabernacle . . . And they shall be joined unto thee, and keep the charge of the tabernacle of the congregation, for all the service of the tabernacle: and a stranger shall not come nigh unto you. And ye shall keep the charge of the sanctuary, and the charge of the altar: that there be no wrath any more upon the children of Israel. And I, behold, I have taken your brethren the Levites from among the children of Israel: to you they are given as a gift for the Lord, to do the service of the tabernacle of the congregation. Therefore thou and thy sons with thee shall keep your priest's office for every thing of the altar, and within the veil; and ye shall serve: I have given your priest's office unto you as a service of gift: and the stranger that cometh nigh shall be put to death (Numbers 18:1–7).

Inasmuch as the Levites did not work for a living, but depended upon the tithes, Moses spelled out just what was to belong to them. Everything—oil, grain, and meat—was to be tithed to support the Levites.

An explanation of the special arrangement was given:

> And the Lord spake unto Aaron, Thou shalt have no inheritance in their land . . . I am thy part and thine inheritance among the children of Israel. And, behold, I have given the children of Levi all the tenth in Israel for an inheritance, for their service which they serve, even the service of the tabernacle of the congregation (Numbers 18:20–21).

The remainder of the chapter, verses 25 to 32, consists of very careful instructions to the Levites to guide them in handling the tithes. And they were told that it was their reward for their service:

> And ye shall bear no sin by reason of it . . . neither shall ye pollute the holy things of the children of Israel, lest ye die (Numbers 18:32).

This study has brought to our minds that the almighty God arranged that they who preached the gospel should live off the gospel. Let us keep in mind that when those who serve in the gospel ministry are paid by the freewill offerings of the church, everything is in order.

NUMBERS 19
Red Heifer

† † †

Did you know that even though an evil deed may be forgiven, the wrongdoer still needs to be cleansed?

In the course of this Old Testament portion instructing the children of Israel as to how they shall act in the land, God's purpose is that His people shall walk in His presence. This is contrary to human nature. It requires a yieldedness and an obedience on their part. Also, they did not know how to do it. No human being would know until God revealed it. Living now in New Testament days, we have the help of the Holy Spirit, who uses various parts of the Scripture to speak to our hearts. But back in those days they had no Scripture. How were they to learn? It was all spelled out carefully as Moses outlined, through Aaron, the high priest.

Just now we shall consider a very important aspect of spiritual life. There are always two aspects when any sin is committed. If a child were told not to step in a mud puddle, but he foolishly played around it and slid in, what would be necessary? Two things must be done: first his disobedience must be dealt with; second, the mud must be washed off. By the same token, guilt must be pardoned, but the stain of the wrongdoing must also be removed. It is wonderfully true, as we read in 1 John 1:9, "If we confess our sins, he is faithful and just to forgive us our sins, and to cleanse us from all unrighteousness."

It is the cleansing we will pay attention to now. Moses instructed Israel to be aware of the need for cleansing. In chapter 19 there is a description of an unusual sacrifice, that of the red heifer.

And the Lord spake unto Moses and unto Aaron, saying, This is
the ordinance of the law which the Lord hath commanded,
saying, Speak unto the children of Israel, that they bring thee a
red heifer without spot, wherein is no blemish, and upon
which never came yoke: and ye shall give her unto Eleazar the
priest, that he may bring her forth without the camp, and one
shall slay her before his face: and Eleazar the priest shall take of
her blood with his finger, and sprinkle of her blood directly
before the tabernacle of the congregation seven times: and one
shall burn the heifer in his sight; her skin, and her flesh, and
her blood, with her dung, shall he burn: and the priest shall
take cedar wood, and hyssop, and scarlet, and cast it into the
midst of the burning of the heifer. Then the priest shall wash
his clothes, and he shall bathe his flesh in water, and afterward
he shall come into the camp, and the priest shall be unclean
until the even. And he that burneth her shall wash his clothes
in water, and bathe his flesh in water, and shall be unclean
until the even. And a man that is clean shall gather up the ashes
of the heifer, and lay them up without the camp in a clean
place, and it shall be kept for the congregation of the children
of Israel for a water of separation: it is a purification for sin
(Numbers 19:1-9).

This is a direct, clear reference to the death of Christ on
Calvary's cross. Our belief in Him is all based upon His
sacrifice for us. Did you notice that the burning of the heifer
was carefully described? All was done in great solemnity with
careful, deliberate, thoughtful obedience. Something was
being done here that was very important. The people would
not necessarily see the connection—that was not important.
This blood of the ashes of the heifer would be used for separation. In any instance where the sin was to be cleansed away, it
would be done with the ashes of the heifer.

And he that gathereth the ashes of the heifer shall wash his
clothes, and be unclean until the even: and it shall be unto the
children of Israel, and unto the stranger that sojourneth among
them, for a statute for ever (Numbers 19:10).

Thus these ashes were provided and stored up for use as a
cleansing agent.

He that toucheth the dead body of any man shall be unclean
seven days. He shall purify himself with it on the third day, and
on the seventh day he shall be clean: but if he purify not
himself the third day, then the seventh day he shall not be
clean. Whosoever toucheth the dead body of any man that is

dead, and purifieth not himself, defileth the tabernacle of the Lord; and that soul shall be cut off from Israel: because the water of separation was not sprinkled upon him, he shall be unclean; his uncleanness is yet upon him. This is the law, when a man dieth in a tent: all that come into the tent, and all that is in the tent, shall be unclean seven days. And every open vessel, which hath no covering bound upon it, is unclean, And whosoever toucheth one that is slain with a sword in the open fields, or a dead body, or a bone of a man, or a grave, shall be unclean seven days. And for an unclean person they shall take of the ashes of the burnt heifer of purification for sin, and running water shall be put thereto in a vessel: and a clean person shall take hyssop, and dip it in the water, and sprinkle it upon the tent, and upon all the vessels, and upon the persons that were there, and upon him that touched a bone, or one slain, or one dead, or a grave: and the clean person shall sprinkle upon the unclean on the third day, and on the seventh day: and on the seventh day he shall purify himself, and wash his clothes, and bathe himself in water, and shall be clean at even. But the man that shall be unclean, and shall not purify himself, that soul shall be cut off from among the congregation, because he hath defiled the sanctuary of the Lord (Numbers 19:11–20).

It was very important that people be cleansed from their uncleanness. This was not just a matter of their physical condition; it was done in that manner in order to teach the people. The cleansing agent had nothing to do with the individual who had sinned.

We do not speak of the ashes of the heifer, but of the blood of the Lord Jesus Christ, which was shed to cleanse our souls.

Many times people will wonder whether a person may be completely forgiven for having done wrong. Any person not only can be forgiven, but he can be completely cleansed, as was done here.

And it shall be a perpetual statute unto them that he that sprinkleth the water of separation shall wash his clothes; and he that toucheth the water of separation shall be unclean until even. And whatsoever the unclean person toucheth shall be unclean; and the soul that toucheth it shall be unclean until even (Numbers 19:21–22).

This was a sober, serious procedure for those people. Everything that was unclean would stay unclean all that day, unless cleansing was effected by taking the ashes of the heifer and sprinkling it upon the person who had been guilty. We should note that the guilt was forgiven because the sacrifice was slain, but the stain was removed by applying the ashes of the red heifer.

That means that if you and I will come humbly before God to confess and forsake our sin in total commitment to Jesus Christ, we can actually count that the sin will be removed. Naaman, the Syrian, who was a leper, was cleansed of his leprosy, and his flesh became again as the flesh of a child. Regardless of the kind of life a person has been living, it is possible for him to be cleansed so that he is whiter than snow in the sight of God.

NUMBERS 20
The Sin of Moses

✝   ✝   ✝

Can you understand why it is vitally important that a servant of the Lord be without sin?

It is easy to overlook the fact that the leaders in spiritual matters are, after all, human beings. But even though a leader has feelings like everyone else, he must control himself because his failures are disastrous. An incident in the Old Testament is classic: the record of the sin of Moses—a great man. We shall see that he sinned in an unusual way. But we know that everyone sins, so it is possible that Moses may have also fallen short of the will of God in many ways that are not recorded.

> Then came the children of Israel, even the whole congregation, into the desert of Zin in the first month: and the people abode in Kadesh; and Miriam died there, and was buried there. And there was no water for the congregation: and they gathered themselves together against Moses and against Aaron. And the people chode with Moses, and spake, saying, Would God that we had died when our brethren died before the Lord! And why have ye brought up the congregation of the Lord into this wilderness, that we and our cattle should die there? And wherefore have ye made us to come up out of Egypt, to bring us in unto this evil place? it is no place of seed, or of figs, or of vines, or of pomegranates; neither is there any water to drink (Numbers 20:1–5).

The Israelites complained the same way we do when we are in trouble, to the people in charge. Here we read what Moses and Aaron did when the people complained:

> And Moses and Aaron went from the presence of the assembly unto the door of the tabernacle of the congregation, and they

111

fell upon their faces: and the glory of the Lord appeared unto them (Numbers 20:6).

God was their refuge, and we should make a note of that. In trouble, in distress, and especially when we are falsely accused, we must remember that God is our refuge, and prayer is our resource. These two men turned to God in prayer, "and the glory of the Lord appeared unto them." Then God gave the instructions to Moses:

> Take the rod, and gather thou the assembly together, thou, and Aaron thy brother, and speak ye unto the rock before their eyes; and it shall give forth his water, and thou shalt bring forth to them water out of the rock: so thou shalt give the congregation and their beasts drink (Numbers 20:7-8).

And then came the disaster:

> And Moses took the rod from before the Lord, as he commanded him. And Moses and Aaron gathered the congregation together before the rock, and he said unto them. Hear now, ye rebels; must we fetch you water out of this rock? And Moses lifted up his hand, and with his rod he smote the rock twice: and the water came out abundantly, and the congregation drank, and their beasts also (Numbers 20:9-11).

Can you notice anything wrong? That is the first and only record we have of Moses talking that way. He lost his temper. He had been told to speak to the rock but he hit the rock twice. The old nature in Moses took over, and with his rod he smote the rock twice. The water came out abundantly: God kept His word.

There is something very important here. A person can do something wrong without having God slap his face immediately. God will follow through and be faithful to His servant, but He will come later to set the record straight.

> And the Lord spake unto Moses and Aaron, Because ye believed me not, to sanctify me in the eyes of the children of Israel, therefore ye shall not bring this congregation into the land which I have given them (Numbers 20:12).

That was a severe judgment, but the judgment of God falls heavier upon those who are nearer to Him. One thing we should note: Moses never complained. He referred to this incident in the Book of Deuteronomy, but he did not accuse

God of being unfair. The higher up a person is, the heavier the blow falls. Those who belong to congregations have pastors and officers, who carry extra responsibility. These leaders are not as free as others. Because of the load that is on them, they must walk carefully.

We see a similar thing happen in the Israelites' coming to the country of Edom, where they made a very humble request that they be allowed to pass through—even offering to pay for the privilege. But Edom refused, with a show of force, saying they would fight to prevent Israel's crossing. "Wherefore Israel turned away from him" (Numbers 20:21). There was no violence: just meek acceptance. But the Scriptures later reveal that the day came when Edom was destroyed, because in that day when their relatives, Israel, asked for help, Edom refused.

> Aaron shall be gathered unto his people: for he shall not enter into the land which I have given unto the children of Israel, because ye rebelled against my word at the water of Meribah (Numbers 20:24).

Aaron was included in the sin of Moses, having agreed with him. His son, Eleazar, was appointed to serve.

> And when all the congregation saw that Aaron was dead, they mourned for Aaron thirty days, even all the house of Israel (Numbers 20:29).

This study has brought something very sobering to our minds. Not many who read these words may be in a position of real responsibility with great authority, but all will be in groups that have leaders. We should keep in mind that those leaders need support.

NUMBERS 21
Brazen Serpent

✝   ✝   ✝

Can you understand how a believer who is walking in the will of God sometimes becomes discouraged?

> And they journeyed from mount Hor by the way of the Red Sea, to compass the land of Edom: and the soul of the people was much discouraged because of the way. And the people spake against God, and against Moses, Wherefore have ye brought us up out of Egypt to die in the wilderness? for there is no bread, neither is there any water; and our soul loatheth this light bread. And the Lord sent fiery serpents among the people, and they bit the people; and much people of Israel died. Therefore the people came to Moses, and said, We have sinned, for we have spoken against the Lord, and against thee; pray unto the Lord, that he take away the serpents from us. And Moses prayed for the people. And the Lord said unto Moses, Make thee a fiery serpent, and set it upon a pole: and it shall come to pass, that every one that is bitten, when he looketh upon it, shall live. And Moses made a serpent of brass, and put it upon a pole, and it came to pass, that if a serpent had bitten any man, when he beheld the serpent of brass, he lived (Numbers 21:4–9).

This story is important because Jesus used it in His teaching, saying, "And as Moses lifted up the serpent in the wilderness, even so must the Son of man be lifted up" (John 3:14). This event began in a very ordinary way. The children of Israel were strangers traveling along over a long road in a foreign land, and they became discouraged. They had a history marked by great events: the deliverance from Egypt; being led continually by a pillar of fire at night and by a cloud in the day; and even being fed manna from heaven. They had been totally dependent upon God, and He had blessed them.

After Mount Sinai, where they were given the law, they had traveled as far as Kadesh-barnea. There they failed to advance, even though God had asked them to go forward. After more than thirty-eight years of wandering in the desert they were defeated, frustrated, and doomed. These were an experienced people: great in victory, and tragic in defeat. Now they were discouraged, because they saw no chance of conditions getting better. All around were sand and desert.

Many of us know what it is to be in situations that seem hopeless. We may not recognize these situations as being the sands of the desert such as the children of Israel traveled over, but we know what it is to see no relief in sight. The people spoke against God and against Moses, accepting no personal responsibility for what was happening to them. They blamed their leaders, tabulating the grounds for their discouragement. They had no milk, no honey, no bread, and no water they could feel sure about. They were fed with manna that fell from heaven, and their souls hated this manna.

God did not argue with them. He just acted. What He did was to send fiery serpents among them. When bitten by these serpents, many of the people died. This was all part of the judgment of God.

The people came to Moses and confessed, "We have sinned." This is the way we can always begin prayer at any time. The one thing that often holds us back from prayer is a sense of our sinfulness, especially if we have some specific wrong. No man needs to turn away from God because of some wrong he has done; he just needs to confess it.

The people then said to Moses, "Pray unto the Lord, that he take away the serpents from us." The Lord told Moses to make a fiery serpent out of brass and put it up on a post in front of everybody. This was not for the good or the strong person, but for anybody who was bitten by a serpent. Anybody who had the feeling that sin was in him, could look at the serpent of brass, and see in that a symbol of the One who would die for them. When they trusted, they found that whoever looked upon the serpent was healed. This is evidence of the grace of God.

In this chapter we also have evidence of the judgment of God. God brought swift judgment upon these people who were arrogantly contemptuous of Him in criticizing Him and His ways. But everyone who looked to the serpent of brass was spared and healed.

So we have here both the judgment and the grace of God. The rest of that chapter tells the story of the destruction of Sihon, the king of the Amorites and of Og, the king of Bashan. Obviously, God blessed the children of Israel as they moved into action and continued on their journey.

NUMBERS 22–24
Balaam

† † †

Do you realize that with God nothing is impossible?

An amazing incident is recorded in Numbers 22, 23 and 24—an attempt by King Balak to bring harm to God's people. No doubt in every nation there is opposition to the ministry of believers. When I first became a believer and made a public profession of faith in the Lord Jesus Christ, I was astonished at the change of attitude on the part of many people. Anyone professing faith in God seems to pose a threat to natural persons and human plans.

There are elements in this story that are altogether remarkable. Israel was an intruder, coming from the outside. I had to learn about that when I first went out as a personal witness for the gospel of the Lord Jesus Christ. I had to understand that if I went up to a certain person and talked to him about the Lord, I was actually threatening to interfere in his affairs. I hoped he would be able to understand that I meant him well. People who carry on personal work as witnesses for Christ need to be very careful that their conduct tells clearly that they mean well.

Israel's coming into this land also made a real difference. In the same way, people who do personal work in witnessing should remember that asking someone to accept the Lord Jesus Christ is asking him to profoundly alter his manner of life.

In this instance Balak was king of the Moabites and known for his wit, cunning, and strength. Israel's progress into the country was known to all, and they appeared invincible. Thus they looked like a threat to the king, and he schemed to thwart their progress. Balaam, the other character in the story, was widely known and acclaimed as a wise man, a prophet. Balak sent for Balaam for help in an interesting way: Balaam was to curse Israel. Balak had respect for Balaam's power, and he wanted Balaam to use it against Israel. Balak's agents came with money to secure the services of Balaam, who turned to God for guidance. God told him plainly: "Thou shalt not go with them; thou shalt not curse the people: for they are blessed" (Numbers 22:12).

Balak persisted, as our enemies do: they come again and again with their temptations. Balak sent another committee with more money and with the promise of great honor. Balaam answered straight out,

> If Balak would give me his house full of silver and gold, I cannot go beyond the word of the Lord my God, to do less or more (Numbers 22:18).

This shows that Balaam had a proper respect for God. Then he went to God in prayer. I am not able to explain what happened. God permitted him to go, but only to work out God's purposes instead of Balak's wishes. In verse 22 there is an astonishing statement, "And God's anger was kindled because he went." God had permitted Balaam to go, but it was not His first choice.

In trying to understand this, it may help to think about God's directive will and God's permissive will. God may have something in mind for me that He wants me to do, but if I insist, He may allow me to do something else. However, He will not like it. This reminds us of a passage in Psalm 106:15, "He gave them their request; but sent leanness into their soul." If a believer in Christ insists on having his own way, he may get God's permission without His approval.

Having received God's permission, Balaam went on his way to go to Balak. But here the record is astonishing. The angel of the Lord stood in his way on the road. The ass Balaam was riding upon saw the angel and ran off the road into the field. Balaam smote the ass and brought him back on the road. Then the angel stood in the path in a narrow place and the ass crowded Balaam's foot against the wall. Balaam smote the ass again. Once more the angel stood in a narrow place and the ass fell down under Balaam. So he smote the ass with his staff. Then, "the dumb ass speaking with man's voice forbade the madness of the prophet" (2 Peter 2:16). Peter explained that Balaam was going to Balak because he loved the wages of unrighteousness. The Lord opened the eyes of Balaam, and the prophet said unto the angel, "I have sinned." The Lord then permitted him to go with this definite restriction, "Only the word that I shall speak unto thee, that thou shalt speak" (Numbers 22:35).

Here is a grave warning for all preachers, teachers, and parents: If we get our desire without God's blessing, His purpose will be accomplished in spite of us. Each attempt by Balaam to do the king's wishes resulted in the prophecy of blessing upon Israel.

When Balak asked Balaam to curse Israel, Balaam opened his mouth and pronounced great blessing upon Israel. The king said, "That is not what I asked you to do." But Balaam again pronounced great blessing upon Israel, finally saying, "Let me die the death of the righteous, and let my last end be like his" (Numbers 23:10). Balak understood that Balaam was actually blessing Israel, when Balaam told the king, "God is not a man, that he should lie; neither the son of man, that he should repent" (Numbers 23:19). Then Balaam told Balak again, "I have received commandment to bless: and he hath blessed; and I cannot reverse it" (Numbers 23:20). And again Balaam said, "All that the Lord speaketh, that I must do" (Numbers 23:26).

What a faithful preacher he was, yet he served the pagan king! It is sobering to realize that I can have my way if I insist upon it, but I will forfeit God's blessing. In that case I will not be able to accomplish anything, because God sets limits upon what I am allowed to do.

NUMBERS 25
Phinehas

† † †

Do you think a believer would ever feel called upon to tolerate open sin?

The Book of Numbers is a compendium of Moses' instructions to guide Israel in practical situations. The record kept for us is also our guidance. In Numbers 25 we face a sober challenge to our hearts as believers. We live in a day of permissiveness and find ourselves pushed to tolerate everything. I raise the question: are we really ever free to tolerate anything? Is drawing the line actually arbitrary discrimination, or is it wholesome and necessary?

Look at ordinary situations in nature as a whole. Can I eat and drink anything I want to? Can I associate with just anybody—a person with smallpox, for instance? Someone may say those illustrations are the exception, but often it is the exception that is very important.

> And Israel abode in Shittim, and the people began to commit whoredom with the daughters of Moab. And they called the people unto the sacrifices of their gods: and the people did eat, and bowed down to their gods. And Israel joined himself unto Baal-peor: and the anger of the Lord was kindled against Israel (Numbers 25:1–3).

Interacting socially with people who are pagan will lead to pagan worship, as it did here.

The Lord's anger brought forth drastic judgment:

> And the Lord said unto Moses, Take all the heads of the people, and hang them up before the Lord against the sun, that the fierce anger of the Lord may be turned away from Israel. And Moses said unto the judges of Israel, Slay ye every one his men that were joined unto Baal-peor (Numbers 25:4–5).

We should note especially the story as it unfolds:

> And, behold, one of the children of Israel came and brought
> unto his brethren a Midianitish woman in the sight of Moses,
> and in the sight of all the congregation of the children of Israel,
> who were weeping before the door of the tabernacle of the
> congregation (Numbers 25:6).

Evidently there was widespread sorrow because of the sin
that was committed, but sorrow over the sin did not make any
difference. Regardless of how sad people may feel about
wrongdoing, the wrong goes on.

> And when Phinehas, the son of Eleazar, the son of Aaron the
> priest, saw it, he rose up from among the congregation, and
> took a javelin in his hand; and he went after the man of Israel
> into the tent, and thrust both of them through, the man of
> Israel, and the woman through her belly. So the plague was
> stayed from the children of Israel. And those that died in the
> plague were twenty and four thousand (Numbers 25:7–9).

There were many people who did not like it when they saw
the evil, and they sorrowed. But the wanton action of an
Israelite became a case in point; and Phinehas rose up, took a
javelin and killed them both.

> And the Lord spake unto Moses, saying, Phinehas, the son of
> Eleazar, the son of Aaron the priest, hath turned my wrath
> away from the children of Israel, while he was zealous for my
> sake among them, that I consumed not the children of Israel in
> my jealousy. Wherefore say, Behold, I give unto him my cove-
> nant of peace: and he shall have it, and his seed after him, even
> the covenant of an everlasting priesthood; because he was zeal-
> ous for his God, and made an atonement for the children of
> Israel (Numbers 25:10–13).

There comes a time when the person who is obedient to God
must act in judgment on that which is evil. The time when
acceptance of evil is widespread is a call for someone to rise up
from the ranks and openly do what God wants done.

Later in the history of Israel, at the time of Gideon, the
enemy took over the whole country and was exacting tribute
from the people, so that they could not even have their own
grain when it was harvested. At that time there were altars to
the evil gods in the very yard of Gideon's father. Gideon
received a commission from the almighty God to gather some

young men together at night to destroy that altar. This Gideon did, knowing it would provoke the enemy and cause trouble. But the trouble was already there; this simply brought it to a head. The people rallied behind Gideon and helped him throw off the enemy.

In the same way, Phinehas reacted against a widespread acceptance of evil, even though it caused death. All this involves a very simple principle: a watchdog must be ready to attack. We may wonder whether any of us will ever be called to be a watchdog. But when evil forces are creeping right into our own homes, it is difficult not to tolerate the evil for the sake of apparent peace and outward quiet.

We should keep in mind that in the case of smallpox we isolate the sick person. We are forced to introduce quarantine, which is a drastic measure. But that is the only way to deal with that disease. The person who knows about it—the watchdog, who can see it all—is the one who must act. At the time that Phinehas acted, no one else was doing anything about it. This young man rose up and did something, once and for all. The result was a great clearing of the air for Israel.

NUMBERS 32
Special Privilege

† † †

Do you understand, since some people have special privileges, what actions we need to take to guard against dissatisfaction among others in the group?

No one in the world is wise enough or strong enough to solve all the problems that may be right there before him. Such problems are increased because of the fact that we all live with others, and it is natural for people to make comparisons. As the apostle Paul said, "For we dare not make ourselves of the number, or compare ourselves with some that commend themselves: but they measuring themselves by themselves, and comparing themselves among themselves, are not wise" (2 Corinthians 10:12).

People are different, and some are better off than others, as were the first two brothers: Cain and Abel. And conditions may be different: some may be rich, and some may be poor; some may be wise, and some may be foolish; some may be strong, and some may be weak; some may be fortunate, and some may be unfortunate. Everywhere there is an unevenness among people as their daily experiences differ.

When we make comparisons among people it can easily arouse envy, eventually leading to hatred, conflict, and contention. When people live with others, unity is necessary. But unity is jeopardized by special privilege. When some people have an advantage, it is hard for others to be satisfied.

Numbers 32 records an incident which demonstrates the solution for this kind of problem. In approaching the land of Canaan, the Israelites came in from the desert side on the east. As they approached the river Jordan, they encountered violent opposition from some pagan people.

When Sihon—king of the Amorites—tried to block their course, God gave Israel the victory; they destroyed Sihon and took his country. Then Og—king of Bashan—tried to stop them, and he also was defeated and destroyed in battle. With Sihon and Og destroyed, the land belonged to the Israelites, and it was good cattle country.

> Now the children of Reuben and the children of Gad had a very great multitude of cattle: and when they saw the land of Jazer, and the land of Gilead, that, behold, the place was a place for cattle; the children of Gad and the children of Reuben came and spake unto Moses, and to Eleazar the priest (Numbers 32:1–2).

They came to speak about this whole matter of the ownership of this land.

> Even the country which the Lord smote before the congregation of Israel, is a land for cattle, and thy servants have cattle: wherefore, said they, if we have found grace in thy sight, let this land be given unto thy servants for a possession, and bring us not over Jordan (Numbers 32:4–5).

Moses realized that granting this request would be a threat to the morale of the other ten tribes.

> And Moses said unto the children of Gad and to the children of Reuben, Shall your brethren go to war, and shall ye sit here? And wherefore discourage ye the heart of the children of Israel from going over into the land which the Lord hath given them? Thus did your fathers, when I sent them from Kadesh-barnea to see the land. For when they went up unto the valley of Eshcol, and saw the land, they discouraged the heart of the children of Israel, that they should not go into the land which the Lord had given them. And the Lord's anger was kindled the same time, and he sware, saying, Surely none of the men that came up out of Egypt, from twenty years old and upward, shall see the land which I sware unto Abraham, unto Isaac, and unto Jacob; because they have not wholly followed me: save Caleb the son of Jephunneh the Kenezite, and Joshua the son of Nun: for they have wholly followed the Lord (Numbers 32:6–12).

Moses reminded them that when the children of Israel as a whole had lost their courage about going into the land, the almighty God had been displeased. Their present request would again discourage Israel as a whole.

And, behold, ye are risen up in your father's stead, an increase
of sinful men, to augment yet the fierce anger of the Lord
toward Israel. For if ye turn away from after him, he will yet
again leave them in the wilderness; and he shall destroy all this
people (Numbers 32:14–15).

Reuben and Gad then proposed a solution:

And they came near unto him, and said, We will build sheep-
folds here for our cattle, and cities for our little ones: but we
ourselves will go ready armed before the children of Israel,
until we have brought them unto their place: and our little ones
shall dwell in the fenced cities because of the inhabitants of the
land. We will not return unto our houses, until the children of
Israel have inherited every man his inheritance. For we will
not inherit with them on yonder side Jordan, or forward; because our inheritance is fallen to us on this side Jordan east-
ward (Numbers 32:16–19).

They offered to undertake special burdens to help the others,
if Moses would permit them to settle there. They would send
their best soldiers to go with the others in the further invasion
of Canaan. Moses told them that they would have to go in the
forefront of the battle, and that those soldiers would have to
stay in the conquering force until all the people were settled
in their places. Then they could come back to enjoy their
privilege. This arrangement proved to be successful.

From this we learn an important practical truth: special
privilege means special responsibility. We believe in the almighty God, but we have to live in this world with our human
differences. Some of us are strong, and some are weak. Here
is the great truth as Paul expressed it:

We then that are strong ought to bear the infirmities of the
weak, and not to please ourselves (Romans 15:1).

Those who are fortunate should undertake special effort on
behalf of the unfortunate; then the morale of a group as a
whole will be sustained.

NUMBERS 35
Cities of Refuge

† † †

Do you realize that compassion for the wrongdoer should include protecting him from hasty judgment, if his crime was not deliberate?

Numbers 35 gives an interesting provision on the part of God's will for His people. The Bible reveals that God has a lively interest in all man's social affairs. God made all men, and He watches over them all. In many people we may not be able to see anything we like. But God loves them all. All human actions are an open book to God, and He is concerned about the weak and innocent, as well as the criminal.

God put upon society the responsibility of administering social control. Sometimes one person is cruel to another person, and sometimes someone even kills another. God laid down this rule: "Whoso sheddeth man's blood, by man shall his blood be shed" (Genesis 9:6).

In this way God places upon society as a whole the responsibility of controlling and restraining the violent and the wicked. In the Old Testament the relatives of the injured party could act for society by reaping vengeance. If one man killed another, the relatives of the murdered man would seek vengeance on the man who had done the wrong. But the impulse for vengeance had to be controlled, not acted upon hastily.

For this precaution, special provisions were set forth in Numbers 35. First, there was a provision for the Levites. They were not to receive any of the land in the country. However, God arranged through Moses that there should be forty-eight cities set aside for their use. Each tribe was to set aside four:

And the cities which ye shall give shall be of the possession of
the children of Israel: from them that have many ye shall give
many; but from them that have few ye shall give few: every one
shall give of his cities unto the Levites according to his inheritance which he inheriteth (Numbers 35:8).

Buried in that we find the principle by which the leader of my
congregation is to be supported. He is to be supported by the
freewill gifts of the congregation. Those who have much will
give much, and those who have less will give less. This is the
way it should be. Our custom of grading salaries contingent
upon relative performance is not biblical.

We notice as we go on in this chapter that there was provision for the person who did wrong unintentionally. This refers
to the involuntary criminal, the person who committed a
crime inadvertently. The Bible prescribes one penalty for
murder—death. But not every case of violent death is the
same. Death resulting from premeditated violence received
the standard penalty. The relatives of the victim acted for
society by seeking vengeance. Their natural impulse to vengeance of course, was to follow through at once. But in the
case of inadvertent death, the slayer was to be free.

Such freedom was secured for him in the City of Refuge.
The relatives would be restrained from harming him there.
These cities were set aside as places of refuge for any uninten-
tional killer. In case of doubt as to his guilt, the people would
examine the evidence of the crime and then decide. If they
judged that the man who committed the crime was innocent
of intent, he would be unharmed. But even then, if he ven-
tured out of the City of Refuge, the avengers could execute
him without penalty. His safety depended upon his staying in
the City of Refuge.

Something about that speaks to our hearts. We have committed sin, and we know that the wages of sin is death. In
most cases the sin we committed was not involuntary; it was
plainly our fault. But God has extended His grace in sending
the Lord Jesus Christ, who is for us a City of Refuge. If we
think of Him that way, we can think of flying to Him for security.
But we must keep one thing in mind: we must stay there.

In order to guard against miscarriage of justice, an interesting rule was set forth.

Whoso killeth any person, the murderer shall be put to death
by the mouth of witnesses: but one witness shall not testify
against any person to cause him to die (Numbers 35:30).

This was a careful safeguard. One witness, even if he saw the
crime, was not enough to bring an accusation that would cause
the other man to die. The scriptural principle is that the
congregation shall judge on the basis of verified evidence, not
on the basis of one man's words.

Throughout the description of these arrangements little attention was paid to personal eminence. It made no difference
who the person was: the one law for each was to be adminis-
tered without favor.

When we think of the careful, meticulous arrangements
that God made on behalf of the man who had unintentionally
done wrong, we can appreciate the wonderful grace of God,
grace that is greater than all our sins.